Steven
SPIELBERG

The Man, His Movies, and Their Meaning

OF RELATED INTEREST FROM

CONTINUUM

American History/American Film, New Expanded Edition, John E. O'Connor and Martin A. Jackson, eds.

American History/American Television, John E. O'Connor, ed.

And the Winner Is . . . The History and Politics of the Oscar Awards, New Expanded Edition, Emanuel Levy

The Cinema of Stanley Kubrick, New Expanded Edition, Norman Kagan

The Dead that Walk: Dracula, Frankenstein, the Mummy, and other Favorite Movie Monsters, Leslie Halliwell

Framework: A History of Screenwriting in the American Film, New Expanded Edition, Tom Stempel

The French through Their Films, Robin Buss

Hitchcock: The First Forty-Four Films, Eric Rohmer and Claude Chabrol

Hitchcock in Hollywood, Joel W. Finler

Italian Cinema: From Neorealism to the Present, New Expanded Edition, Peter Bondanella

Loser Take All: The Comic Art of Woody Allen, New Expanded Edition, Maurice Yacowar

A Project for the Theatre, Ingmar Bergman

The Screening of America: Movies and Values from Rocky *to* Rain Man, Tom O'Brien

Screening Space: The American Science Fiction Film, Vivian Sobchack

Small-Town America in Film: The Decline and Fall of Community, Emanuel Levy

Storytellers to the Nation: A History of American Television Writing, Tom Stempel

Take 22: Moviemakers on Moviemaking, Judith Crist

Teleliteracy: Taking Television Seriously, David Bianculli

Toms, Coons, Mulattoes, Mammies, and Bucks: An Interpretive History of Blacks in American Films, New Expanded Edition, Donald Bogle

World Cinema since 1945: An Encyclopedic History, William Luhr, ed.

For more information on these and other titles on the performing arts or literature, write to:

Continuum
370 Lexington Avenue
New York, NY 10017

Steven
SPIELBERG

The Man, His Movies, and Their Meaning

PHILIP M. TAYLOR

CONTINUUM/NEW YORK

For my mother, Hilda,
who introduced me to her lifelong obsession,
the cinema,
and my father, Alex,
who tolerated it on his return from war

1992
The Continuum Publishing Company
370 Lexington Avenue, New York, NY 10017

Copyright © 1992 by Philip M. Taylor

Printed in Great Britain
by Butler & Tanner Ltd, Frome, Somerset

Library of Congress Cataloging-in-Publication Data

Taylor, Philip M.
    Steven Spielberg : the man, his movies, and their
meaning / Philip M. Taylor.
        p.   cm.
    Includes bibliographical references and index.
    ISBN 0-8264-0615-7
    1. Spielberg, Steven, 1947– . I. Title.
PN1998.3.S65T39   1992
791.43'0233'092—dc20
    [B]   92-10212
                                                          CIP

Contents

Preface and Acknowledgements

Writing about films and filmmaking has generally fallen into three broad categories. First, there are the memoirs and autobiographies written by participants. These may throw informative light on the workings of the film industry but they are more usually designed to vindicate the careers and reputations of the people doing the writing. Second, there are the often sensationalist books and biographies written for the general film fan. Finally, there are the academic monographs. These generally analyse film by reference to a form and language that is difficult for general readers to penetrate. This book attempts in some ways to take something from all three categories by informatively yet unsensationally examining the life and work of Steven Spielberg, where possible in his own words, and with a jargon-free critical analysis which general readers and film fans will be able to understand.

Commercial filmmaking is a collaborative business. The director is like the captain of a ship, and determines its course, speed and overall mood. He is in turn answerable to the ship's or studio's owners. In the last ten years, Spielberg has become both captain and shipowner thanks to his unassailable position within the Hollywood hierarchy. This would appear to make him an even more suitable topic for what academics have termed the *auteur* theory of film analysis. Even before he became a movie mogul with the establishment of Amblin Entertainment in 1984, Spielberg was still very much in control of the films that had put him in that position, though he was quick to eschew *auteuristic* interpretations. For example, he is on record as saying:

> I believe everything begins with the writer's concept. For a movie even to
> be made, somebody has to be attracted enough to the writer's script to say

'I commit X number of dollars to this'. The minute a director starts working on it, it becomes another individual's concept. He becomes the creative ramrod. I think there should be – if the movie succeeds – a kind of shared credit. If it's a big failure then it's the director's own fault. And when a director writes his own script, as I did for *Close Encounters of the Third Kind*, it's still a collaborative art . . . You've got a cameraman, a special effects man, even publicity people who make tremendous contributions to the success – or failure – of a film. I'll tell you how – really, the only way – I see myself becoming an *auteur* is when I pick up my 8mm camera and shoot my girl watching television.

Again, at the 1974 Cannes film festival he said: 'Those directors who believe in the *auteur* theory will have coronaries at an early age. You can't play all the instruments at once.' While accepting the validity of Spielberg's own determination to give credit where credit is due on his films, this book will concentrate mainly on the particular instrument he himself plays with such virtuosity as a director whose popular appeal is unparalleled in the history of the movies.

Writing, like filmmaking, is a creative process that could not be completed successfully without the help of a whole host of individuals whose contribution is as essential as the author's but whose input rarely receives the same kind of recognition. I am delighted, therefore, to acknowledge here the help I have received from numerous individuals in the research and writing of this book. For her substantial contribution to the gathering of appropriate printed materials, I am especially indebted to Debbie Whitaker. Nor could I fail to acknowledge the help of Gail Holder and the staff of the Headingley (Leeds) branch of Ritz Video Film Hire (Scotland) Ltd for their help in acquiring all the necessary visual materials. Ian Bromner and Maz Brook were also quick to volunteer their services as research assistants. The staff of the Inter-Library Loans Service at the University of Leeds' Brotherton Library were their customary helpful selves. Nicholas Pronay Senior and Nicky Pronay Junior respectively provided the professional support and interpretational input so essential to the completion of a project such as this. My brother, Alex, together with Jackie Slater and Sue Heward, deserve the highest recognition for their tolerance thresholds in not allowing the tapping of a laptop computer to disturb the tranquillity of their summer holiday in the South of France. For encouraging me to continue with writing a book so different from the kind I have been used to, I am finally indebted to Sandra Billingham, Sally Benson and Fiona Assersohn and all those other friends who shared with me bouts of uncontrollable tear-shedding during the course of the research and writing.

I would also like to thank the British Film Institute Stills, Posters and Designs department and the Joel Finler Collection for the photographs, which were originally issued to publicise or promote films or TV material made or distributed by the following companies, to whom I gratefully offer acknowledgement: Amblin, Columbia Pictures, Cinema International Corporation, Hollywood Pictures, Lucasfilm, MGM, Paramount Pictures Corporation, SLM Entertainment, Sony Pictures Entertainment, Tristar Pictures, Universal, Universal City Studios Inc., UIP, Warner Bros.

Introduction

> For thousands of years society had the idea of creating cultural heroes: people you could look up to, who *were* idealized so that we could aspire to be like them. But in contemporary culture that doesn't exist; especially in the media, the idea is rampant that everybody must be torn down, that nobody is really any good. From my point of view, that's a sick culture. To take someone like John Lennon apart completely disregards the contributions he made to society, and says to everybody, 'Don't even *bother* to do anything.' It's a sad situation when you can't have a hero without feet of clay. And there's now a very limited view of what's acceptable in art; if you do something a little more offbeat, nobody will have anything to do with it.

Thus spake George Lucas in 1989. The director of *Star Wars* (1977) and great friend of Steven Spielberg, was referring to a phenomenon that has come to afflict our greatest contemporary popular artists, namely one in which mass popularity somehow generates critical contempt. Steven Spielberg, the most commercially successful filmmaker of the past 20 years, indeed, in the entire history of Hollywood, is no exception to that unfortunate rule.

This might surprise those millions of people worldwide who eagerly await his next production and flock to see his films. Films bearing the stamp: 'Steven Spielberg' will automatically attract mass audiences, whether they be directed by Spielberg himself or by one of his protégés. He is the Director–Producer as Star, having assumed a status in the eyes of the cinema-going public that arouses a level of audience expectation more typically associated with movie actors and actresses from the golden age of Hollywood.

For someone so personally unassuming and unpretentious operating within the pressurized economic and egocentric climate of Hollywood, this might seem an unbearable weight to shoulder. But Spielberg carries his star status with modesty and magnanimity. He is a man virtually unspoiled by success. However, although his achievements have brought him great personal wealth and professional power, they have also created for him something of a creative straitjacket. For example, the level of expectation concerning the entertainment value of his work is such that he is under enormous pressure from producers and audiences alike to repeat a proven formula rather than branch out into newer, perhaps riskier, directions. Moreover, he has set such a high standard for himself that the slightest detected drop in profits or performance is greeted with an exaggerated and almost gloating reaction that the golden boy has lost his Midas touch. Yet he remains a man who has simply been blessed with the opportunity of making a living out of what he has always wanted to do most – telling stories on film.

He claims not to be particularly interested in the views of critics, which is perhaps just as well considering how many seem to hover over him like hawks waiting to move in for the kill at the slightest sign of weakness or failure. 'I just make the kind of films that I would want to see,' he has said. His priority remains 'what the audience has to say, because I have always felt that I have always worked for the audience more than anybody else. Those are my bosses.' He can therefore draw comfort from his commercial success so long as the people he cares most about continue to pay to see and enjoy the fruits of his labours, although one suspects he still craves the elusive critical acclaim afforded to many of his filmmaking friends and contemporaries. 'I think Hollywood will forgive me once I'm 55,' he has joked. 'I don't know *what* they'll forgive me for, but they'll forgive me when I'm 55.'

Spielberg is a man steeped in film culture and film history. He is as much a part of the audience as any devoted filmgoer. This helps to explain why his films contain so many references to other films, which is both entertaining for the filmbuff and reassuring for the casual observer. This is because Spielberg never assumes that his audience operates within a vacuum. He always attempts to relate his stories to audience experiences, whether of real life or of the fantasy world of the movies. He presents his films as just the latest in a long line of actual and cinematic influences, and his success derives largely from his ability to identify with and exploit those experiences. He himself watches everything, although his favourite periods are the first and last two decades of sound films: 'I'm really interested in films from around 1933 to 1954. And then I sort of go off films for a while – you know, from the mid-fifties until the early seventies.' This is a telling admission in that he eschews the films made

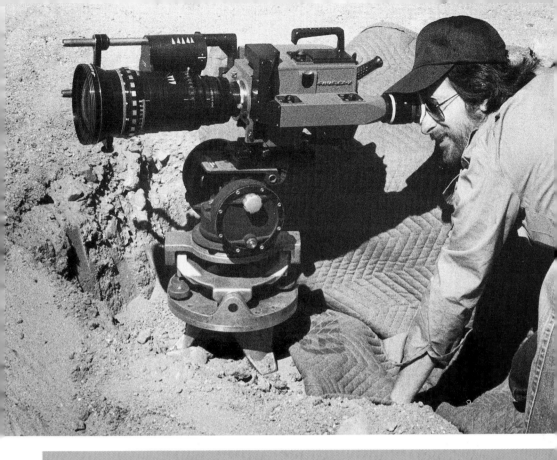

Spielberg where he most likes to be: behind the camera, in 1980.

during the time he was growing up, those made during the very period of his own life from which he constantly draws for most of his own films made as an adult.

As we shall see, the cinema was not Steven Spielberg's most formative influence. That place, in so far as any medium is concerned, belongs to television. Yet television represents for Spielberg only one (admittedly significant) facet of an upbringing that was in many respects typical of post-World War Two American suburban consumer affluence. Television sets, like motor cars and refrigerators, were a symbolic indication of social success in the minds of middle or suburban America of the 1950s. They provided a window on to all sorts of worlds through which children could extend and exploit their imaginations. Their parents' drive to comfort and conformism often brought with it dislocation and divorce, and doubtless contributed to the disillusioned backlash of the 1960s generation. Spielberg the boy was very much part of that background, a victim of it as well as a beneficiary once it resurfaced in his films made as an adult. Spielberg became so obsessed with his imagination that he took refuge in escapism rather than joining in the political and societal aspirations of many of his contemporaries. It is almost as though as the man he seized upon the chance to relive what he saw as a comparatively unhappy childhood and then to reorder it on film.

His films therefore reflect the era that formed the dominant ideology of his generation, which in turn explains their success amongst audiences steeped in those same influences.

Spielberg is very much a product of his times, but he is also a moulder of them. In the age of television, he has done more than any other individual to encourage people away from the influence of the 'tube of plenty' and back to the cinema. Whether Spielberg can continue to do this as he passes into what is called his more 'mature' phase was a matter of much debate as this book was being written. Whether he succeeds or not, however, he has already made a sufficient mark on the history of the cinema to merit a serious evaluation of his influences and achievements to date.

Despite his undisputed position in the history of the cinema, remarkably little serious attention has been paid to Spielberg in print. Reviewing one of the most recent studies, by Mott and Saunders, George Kimball wrote: 'I realize, of course, that Spielberg is a new subject and that in the hard world of academic criticism [the] first one into the pond usually winds up playing sitting duck for a lot of cranky shoreline snipers.' The present study is designed for those general readers and filmgoers who wish to know a little bit more about a man whose movies have provided them with such pleasure.

Spielberg's extraordinary popularity with the public is, as mentioned, frequently matched by the extraordinary amount of critical hostility that he and his films have attracted. Of *E.T. – The Extra Terrestrial* (1982), for example, the most commercially successful film ever made and widely admired by even the most hard-hearted of film reviewers, Kenneth Robinson wrote that it was 'the worst film I have ever seen . . . nauseating, sentimental rubbish'. Derek Malcolm, the respected film critic of the *Guardian*, who admires Spielberg's filmmaking skills generally, has none the less expressed concern at what he sees as a lack of substance:

> Magical as he often is, there's a weightlessness there too. He is often about as profound as a cowpat, especially at moments when he's aiming for profundity . . . Spielberg substitutes brilliant, burnished technique for proper thought, and manipulative skill for proper passion. He can make us

laugh and cry to order, but you can't take anything but the memory of it out of the theatre.

With compliments like this, who needs detractors? The same sort of reluctant admiration at times descends into downright contempt. Kenneth Anger's famous if enigmatic short review of *Close Encounters of the Third Kind* (1977) is typical of the sting-in-the-tail approach:

> Why have I been to see *Close Encounters of the Third Kind* six times, braving lines, cold, and four-buck-fifty admission price?
>
> Can it be love of the movie? Listen, I have been back to see *Close Encounters of the Third Kind* six times to see if I have been ripped off. I mean. *Scorpio Rising*. The toys, the kid. I mean. *Lucifer Rising*. The saucers. Subject dear to my heart.
>
> Other movies that have ripped off Kenneth Anger, *American Graffiti* (music), *Electra Glide in Blue* (theme) I've stayed away from. Not *Close Encounters of the Third Kind*. I've been back to see it six times.
>
> Then there's the matter of my name (abbreviated) on the track. There it is, *Dolbyized, and it sounds just like kenanger* in the burst of static at the start of the Indianapolis control room scene.
>
> Is that punk hustler Spielberg trying to tell me something, like: Haw, haw, ripped you off!??!

I am tempted to conclude that such antipathy says more about reviewers' prejudices and personalities than it does about the films themselves. When *Time* magazine wrote in 1982 that 'Spielberg is the kind of American, extremely intelligent and utterly unintellectual, who can baffle Europeans', it might well have added 'and critics'.

Fortunately, Spielberg is more than willing to discuss what *he* is trying to achieve in his films rather than simply allowing others a free hand when it comes to their interpretation. When asked, for example, how he felt about the popularity of his work, he replied, almost as if looking back to Anger:

> It's sort of interesting how that works. I didn't make *E.T.* to be popular. I didn't make *Close Encounters of the Third Kind* to be popular. We made *Raiders* [*of the Lost Ark* (1981)] to be popular, but not *The Color Purple* [1985]. I've been as surprised as anybody else when the results are greater than I ever dreamed possible. People begin to get suspicious of your intentions when the films are so wildly popular. Of all my 'megahits', so to speak, everybody loves the movie for the first few months, and then when its starts breaking records, someone'll say, 'Well, wait a second. I'm being tricked. There's some kind of evil seduction afoot. I don't trust that

Spielberg. He's manipulating me now. I know, I enjoyed it, I saw it four times, but that little bastard manipulated me!' I just have to separate myself from all that, otherwise I'd start believing only the bad publicity. And I'd never make another film.

When, early in 1990, Barry Norman interviewed Spielberg for BBC television, he asked him about some of the vicious reviews of *Always* (1989), suggesting that it was almost as though some people were willing disaster upon him. Spielberg replied:

> If I really wanted to take reviews seriously, I'd show my films to all the critics in rough-cut so at least if they wanted to take me over the coals they could then. But [if] there was one good idea I could make the change. I'm very generous about that kind of thing. But we don't do that, so I just don't really bother myself with reviews. I read reviews sometimes a year later.

When pressed further about why he thought he attracted so much criticism, he replied in typically gracious terms:

> All it took was *Jaws* to be this big hit in 1975 and then there were some people who went after *Close Encounters of the Third Kind* as if I had murdered their entire family. Friends would support me and slap me on the back and say it was this or it's that, you were too successful at too early an age, but I just think it's the nature of the business. Some people tend to be more creative writing negative, vitriolic sentences as opposed to writing glowing reports and my feeling is that everybody has a right to their opinion. [If] it becomes personal and they border on malice and defamation of character, then I would take exception, but until it borders on complete defamation of character it's just their job. You know, I've got my job, they've got their job – and I'm glad I have my job.

Spielberg was conscious of people wanting him to fail right at the start of his career when he was first employed as a television director by Universal Studios in 1969 at the age of 21. Then, he appeared to be a precocious innocent in a world of hardened veterans as he encountered all the prejudices that a previous *wunderkind*, Orson Welles, had experienced 30 years earlier. He was a young man in a hurry, driven by a burning ambition to enter the entertainment world that had been his primary means of escape as an adolescent. 'I was on the outside of a wonderful hallucination that everyone was sharing,' he said. 'And I wanted to do more than be a part of the hallucination. I wanted to control it. I wanted to be a director.' He had felt this from at least the age of 12 when he first began to make short home movies. Then, in 1969, on the basis of skills displayed in a 22-minute short film, *Amblin'* (after which he was to name his own production company in 1984), Universal television gave him a remarkable and unprecedented opportunity. He was taken on board with a unique seven-year contract, making him the youngest director ever to have been signed up by a major Hollywood studio on a longterm basis. He has dominated commercially successful American filmmaking ever since.

Another remarkable aspect of the negative response to Spielberg's success is that he (like Welles) has never won an Oscar from the Academy of Motion Picture Arts and Sciences (AMPAS) for his achievements as a director. He and his films have been nominated several times, yet he was bypassed in 1975 when *Jaws* was beaten by *One Flew Over the Cuckoo's Nest* and Milos Forman, in 1977 when *Close Encounters of the Third Kind* for which Spielberg was nominated Best Director was beaten by *Annie Hall* and Woody Allen, in 1981 when *Raiders of the Lost Ark* was defeated by *Chariots of Fire* and by Warren Beatty (as the director of *Reds*) and again in 1982 when *E.T.* was defeated by *Gandhi* and Richard Attenborough. Unlucky, perhaps in that he was up against some marvellous competition, but there seemed to be something more to it than that.

The Color Purple won 11 nominations in 1985 – but not one for its director, a conspicuous affront to any director in that position but especially so in light of Spielberg's considerable personal courage in making an all-black film. As it turned out, the film failed to win a single statuette – and it is the only example in film history of a director who had already won the Directors Guild of America award for a film not even earning an Oscar nomination. Quite understandably, this hurt him. Warner Brothers took the unprecedented step of issuing a public statement that 'the company is shocked and dismayed that the movie's primary creative force, Steven Spielberg, was not recognized'. Clint Eastwood, who himself was to emerge in the seventies and eighties as a director of considerable talent with no Oscars, wondered whether it was because Spielberg was 'a little too young and too successful. He has done so well, it may be a long time before anyone bestows on him any brasswork'. Other nations have at least proved more generous than his own in recognizing his art.

Surely it can't simply be a matter of jealousy? Americans, after all, pride themselves on loving a winner. The Directors Guild of America has honoured Spielberg on numerous occasions. In 1988, when the groundbreaking *Who Framed Roger Rabbit?* failed to secure any Oscar nomination, Spielberg's co-producers at Disney's Touchstone Pictures joked that the film's chances 'suffered from the three S's: success, special effects and Spielberg'. There is certainly an element of Hollywood snobbery about special effects films, with which Spielberg has unfairly come to be identified. The same resentment tends to be applied to box-office successes. But neither explains *The Color Purple* snub, a less successful Spielberg film (comparatively) with little or no special effects. David Lewin of The Daily Mail investigated the issue at the time of *The Color Purple* controversy and claimed that 'the main reason is that his attitudes and his success are based upon simple certainties which more sophisticated minds cannot – or will not – accept' and that 'Middle America . . . is something Beverly Hills does not understand'. Perhaps the feeling is also that Spielberg's films had already been rewarded enough by their commercial success, or even that his work poses a threat to the Movie Establishment because Spielberg demystifies the art of filmmaking by producing one success after another. Can it really be that easy? Well, of course not, but Spielberg does seem to possess something that others would like to have but no one else can either reproduce or recreate so consistently. And when critics look for complexity, they find simplicity, which confuses and irritates them. Spielberg himself says, 'in a way, it's a high compliment; it means they care enough *not* to give it to me'.

Despite these repeated snubs, and despite being awarded the Irving G. Thalberg Award for continued production excellence in 1986 by the American Motion Picture Academy, he himself would still love to win a director's Oscar. Which true film fan would not? Indeed, he almost came close with *Rain Man*, which he was supposed to make with Tom Cruise and Dustin Hoffman (with whom he had wanted to work ever since seeing *The Graduate* in 1967 and with whom he was finally able to work in 1991 with *Hook*). He did in fact spend five months on the script but had to hand over to Barry Levinson in view of a prior commitment to George Lucas to make the third Indiana Jones film. Even here, Spielberg doubts whether *Rain Man* would have done so well at the Oscars if his name had been on it:

> When the film began winning Best Picture, Best Writer, I kept thinking 'God, maybe I should have forgotten my entire friendship with George Lucas and said George, go and hire somebody else to do Indy 3 and I should have done that.' But then I also thought realistically that I have a very strange relationship with Hollywood and practically speaking if my name had been on the *Rain Man*, shot for shot what Barry had done, simply if my name had been substituted for his, I probably in my heart of hearts don't think I would even have been nominated as director on that film and I'm not sure the film would have won that many awards . . . I think that I bring to a movie a lot of baggage . . . and a lot of people can't quite see me making those leaps of both faith and style transition.

Generosity is a Spielberg hallmark. He has many friends within the industry (though obviously not in the Motion Picture Academy), is active in directors' guilds for all the right sort of causes (especially his fight against colorization and his attempt to save Cannon Elstree Studios) and he is keen to help talented filmmakers. In 1989, he got together with another friend, Martin Scorsese, to finance the restoration of David Lean's 1962 classic, *Lawrence of Arabia*, threatening, so the story goes, never to make a film for Columbia again unless this was done. That whole exercise 'made me feel like going back to film school. One of the most intimidating things for anybody who takes himself seriously as a filmmaker is to sit in that theatre and realize that so many of us have so far to go before we're able to recreate even seven moments in a masterwork like that'.

Despite his contributions to the welfare of the film industry, however, Spielberg remains the victim of the most ungenerous judgements. Henry Jaglom, for example, an art-film director and voting member of the Academy who, despite the fact that very few people have even heard of him or his films, has been a constant critic of Spielberg and has said: 'There is a place for mass entertainment, but it shouldn't be confused with art or quality award-winning filmmaking.' The overall view that appears to be prevalent within certain parts of the movie establishment is that mass appeal is no indication of artistic merit; that those who have achieved both, such as Chaplin and Hitchcock, have done so only erratically – which is their salvation – but that Spielberg is different because he is reasonably consistent in his success, which somehow automatically precludes him from ever attaining creative integrity. It is, in short, an arrogant and elitist attitude that is patronizing to audience tastes and insulting to a master craftsman.

Perhaps Spielberg is not taken seriously by an intellectual or critical elite because his films are not about 'serious' subjects. They are about fantasy and innocence, rather than about reality and substance. And these are not the sort of subjects that immediately attract the interests of serious critics or commentators who characteristically take themselves far too seriously. Such people also tend to regard cinema as a higher form of art than television and Spielberg is very much a product of the television age and therefore, by definition, a creature of a much lower order. A more sympathetic Martin Amis has said of him:

TV is popular art. Spielberg is a popular artist who has outstripped but not outgrown the medium that shaped him. Like Disney – and, more remotely, like Dickens – his approach is entirely non-intellectual, heading straight for the heart, the spine, the guts.

Spielberg, then, has been a victim of his own preoccupation with emotion and of his non-intellectual approach, much as Orson Welles was (and who once said that 'the film director should be very intelligent, preferably not intellectual – because the intellectual is the enemy of all the performing arts').

In 1985, still reeling from the Oscar snub, Spielberg conceded that he had perhaps been a little too formulaic in his early approach:

> After *E.T.* people expected a certain kind of film from me, a certain amount of screams and cheers and laughs and thrills. And I was caving in to that. I knew I could give it to them, but I realise it made me a little arrogant about my own style. It was all too easy. The whole titillation I've always felt about the unknown – of seeing that tree outside my bedroom window and shutting the drapes till morning – was taken away from me. And I got scared. I don't want to see where I'm going.

And although Spielberg was to recover from his personal setbacks with productions such as *Who Framed Roger Rabbit?* and films directed such as *Indiana Jones and the Last Crusade* (1989), some would argue that he has been unable to recapture his earlier form. Even he has said 'you don't really improve so much as you get more courageous. So it's not really a question of getting better because, looking at it subjectively, I think some of my earlier films are better than some of my later ones.'

Hostile criticism does tend to create in him momentary lapses of self-confidence. However, when people choose to highlight his allegedly most spectacular flop – *1941*, made in 1979 at a cost of $27 million – they should bear in mind that it eventually recouped $23.4 million in the United States, while overseas rentals actually helped it to break even. With more failures like that, Hollywood would be in a far healthier position financially. In 1985, drawing some comfort from his financial security (his personal wealth is incalculable) and from the recent establishment of Amblin Entertainment, he said: 'Yeah, I'm a mogul now. And I love work the way Patton loved the stink of battle. But when I grow up I still want to be a director.' With more dedicated director-producers like him, Hollywood would be in a far healthier position creatively.

Spielberg is himself characteristically self-deprecating about his own work: 'I can dump on me better than anybody else.' He used to be quite defensive about his work being compared to his contemporaries and friends (the so-called 'Movie Brats'), including Francis Ford Coppola and Martin Scorsese. 'I don't paint in the strong browns and greens of Francis, or in Marty's sombre greys and whites,' he has said. 'Francis makes films about power and loyalty, Marty makes films about paranoia and rage. I use primary colours, pastel colours.' The view of Scorsese,

Elliott (Henry Thomas) sees the approaching lights of the men looking for E.T. in *E.T. The Extra-Terrestial*, 1982.

whom he first met in 1971, is that the audience sees Spielberg's name on a project 'and expects more and bigger. That's a tough position to be in.' Coming from a director whose reputation as one of America's foremost 'serious' directors also serves as a yardstick by which his next film is judged, Scorsese knows what he is talking about. But Spielberg has also admitted that he doesn't take enough chances with his films and, in 1982, planned to come out of his 'pyrotechnic stage' and examine what he called 'the darker side of my make-up'. What he meant, he said six years later, was that:

> When I see a movie like *Raging Bull* that I know I could never make the way Marty [Scorsese] can make it and I say that would be a risk for me . . . I'm talking about a personal challenge and I haven't tried it because I'm not Marty. I know I couldn't make *Raging Bull* one-tenth as powerful or as quixotic as Marty was able to make it. I know I'm not a hard guy. I know that I have a dark side, but I don't have a real dark side.

Spielberg enjoys talking about the 'dark side', perhaps as a result of long conversations with his great friend Lucas, whose *Star Wars* trilogy has the struggle between the forces of darkness and light as its central motif. He also, one suspects, likes to tease journalists with stories and observations that can often appear contradictory. For example, he once told Bianca Jagger and Andy Warhol in a 1982 interview:

> The kinds of movies that don't reach me are *noir* European cinema. For some reason I've never been touched by *film noir* or trauma drama, psychodrama, anything having to do with the deep human condition. I've had a tough time understanding cerebral movies. I try. I go to everything.

But Spielberg has continued to wrestle with this issue (or tease interviewers with it), perhaps prompted by continued attacks that his films are about trite subjects. His admission that he has a little darkness in him is evident in many of the horror aspects of his films and was further qualified during the final stages of Amblin's *Arachnophobia* (1990) about which he said:

> I love this kind of nightmare. I like to feel my skin crawling under my shirt trying to get up to my jugular vein. I'm diabolical in that sense. I get perverse pleasure in making people sweat in their underwear. It doesn't make me the nicest guy in the world but I sure enjoy it.

The majority of his films have, after all, contained strong hints of something evil – from the Great White Shark in *Jaws* through to the Thuggies and Nazis in the 'Indiana Jones' trilogy – which allows him to examine his darker side, although goodness and virtue always triumph over evil and cynicism in the end.

Spielberg has always remained a romantic storyteller rather than a prophet of doom. His films naturally reflect the psychology and sensibilities of the man at the time they were made and, like all creative people, his insecurities and priorities fluctuate. He is also growing in confidence all the time. As he progressed through the age of 40, he began to consider future directions, saying in 1990: 'Could I have made *Raging Bull* the way Marty made *Raging Bull*? Two years ago, I would have said no. Today I would say "Yes, I would". That's the difference.' Even so, although he worked on the preparatory stages of *Cape Fear* (1991), a project which interested him because of its emphasis on the family, he handed over to Scorsese who directed one of Amblin's first dark psycho-thrillers. Instead Spielberg chose to make *Hook*.

Given that Spielberg's films so often draw on his own experiences of growing up in conventional middle-class American suburban communities, where families have been affected by divorce or estrangement, it might appear surprising that such a quintessentially American filmmaker should so greatly admire British filmmaking, especially its crews – 'the best in the world' – not to mention British directors. David Lean, for example, was 'the greatest influence I ever had'. Commenting on *Lawrence of Arabia, Bridge on the River Kwai* (1957) and *Great Expectations* (1946), he has said: 'all his pictures have small, intimate stories, and large-scale telling'. Powell and Pressburger's *The Red Shoes* (1948) 'is one of the most important films of my life' and he also thought their *A Canterbury Tale* (1944) 'a wonderful picture'. And, of course, Alfred Hitchcock, from whom he borrows heavily in many of his horror touches and with whom he has often been compared. Quite simply, he says:

> I've been so influenced by craft. And it just happens that those movies I have been most influenced by are stamped 'Made in Britain'. Even though the British film industry doesn't exist as it used to be, the filmmakers are still there. I keep wondering, why is it that the British film is so marvellous for me? I think it's because they're careful. A British film is as carefully made as a fine shotgun from Purdey. Every part is hand-tooled.

At least with this attitude he could draw some comfort from losing out at the Oscars to *Chariots of Fire* and *Gandhi*.

Until Spielberg produces a body of 'adult' or 'dark' work that critics can relate to more effectively, they will remain frustrated by him. Perhaps they have spent too much time revelling in the darkness of Bergman and Buñuel? Spielberg has commented that if audiences of the 1990s want the mood and dark humour of such films as *Batman*, 'I might as well pack it in, because I'm not able to do those kind of movies. They don't appeal to me at all. I also never pander to an audience. If that's going to be the trend, then I'm going to have to find an alternative occupation.' The success of *Batman* in America totally confounded him. He admired its look and its performances but he couldn't understand why its dark, broody, cynical feel swept all his films, with the exception of *E.T.*, further down the all-time charts. '*Batman* was a triumph of production and design and atmosphere . . . But, aside from Nicholson and the sets, I didn't get it. And by not getting it, but with the rest of America getting it – although Europe didn't get it like America did – I thought: well, maybe I'm out of touch.' Despite his repeated assertion that it is impossible to read national mood swings, Spielberg suspected that he had lost his instinctive ability to provide the audience with the films it wanted to see. In the end, he only makes the kind of films *he* wants to make (refusing, for example, to make a *Jaws* sequel, with a consequent glaring drop in the quality of those follow-ups), and his ability thus far to sense what his audiences want is nothing short of uncanny.

Yet there remains a view that the success of Spielberg's allegedly simplistic films about innocence had somehow caused a terminal rot in the American filmmaking industry. He is accused of creating the 1980s' trend of teen-movies, all of which were admittedly less effective imitations of Spielberg's supposedly limited style and substance. True, there were many cheap and nasty imitations, but this does seem to miss an important point about changes in the structure of the American motion-picture industry, particularly caused by economic pressures. Blaming Spielberg, as Barry Norman put it, 'for less talented and more mercenary people coldly ripping off his work is grossly unfair'.

Spielberg's own analysis on this point is that there are insufficient numbers of well-trained people either emerging from the film schools or sufficiently steeped in film history or who have spent enough time making films on their own and learning their craft through experience. To help rectify this, Spielberg has made substantial donations to the University of Southern California's film programme. Moreover, he feels that only very few actors prove capable of making the transition to behind the camera (he cites Robert Redford and Warren Beatty as examples). But the main problem, he feels, is the dearth of first-class screenwriters. He admits that he himself does not have a sufficiently literate background – his own education was visual – and when receiving the Thalberg award he appealed to the industry to promote a talent that he himself admits to lacking:

> Every time now that I write something down, and then am able to recall the film where a form of that idea may have come from, I immediately throw it out – because I am embarrassed.

In fact, Spielberg has been criticized in some quarters for holding on to the film rights for books he has bought without actually converting them into films (*Schindler's Ark* being one example). But the main problem facing the movie industry as a whole is one that happens not to be shared by Spielberg. Because of economic pressures arising from the mounting cost of filmmaking – on average $20-25 million per movie at the time of writing – the industry has become too cautious, which means that risk-taking movies are unlikely to be made unless huge financial returns

Spielberg as Executive Producer and Joe Dante as Director on the set of *Gremlins*, 1984. The film is a movie buff's paradise, containing scores of references to other movies including some of Spielberg's formative influences, such as Walt Disney and Frank Capra.

can be guaranteed. This is why publicity hype often costs as much as it does actually to make a film. And although Spielberg has also been criticized for not taking enough chances making films of a different kind to those he has proven he can make successful, he says:

> It's funny, the term risky. My idea of risky is what I can test myself with, what I can challenge myself with. But in Hollywood it means what I will commit to which doesn't make any money. I feel I have a responsibility to myself more than to the film community. I know that sounds very arrogant, but I can't suddenly think about being a leader, hoping that they will follow me away from the trend I am credited with or accused of beginning, with the E.T.'s and Raiders and the big successful pictures.

Being more fortunate than most, he is now able to act comparatively independently in terms of his film projects. But he never forgets his own experiences or underestimates the difficulties others have to undergo in the harsh economic climate of contemporary Hollywood. Ever since 1941, 'my encounter with economic reality', he has felt a sense of responsibility to the film community as well as to himself. As the vastly under-rated Heaven's Gate (1980) demonstrated, corporations can fall too readily with an expensive box-office flop. Spielberg's solution is simple: 'If each studio would take $1 million profit per big movie and invest it in film schools and writing programs, we'd have the industry that David O. Selznick and Irving Thalberg created.'

Spielberg does what he can to help. Describing himself as an 'independent movie-maker working within the Hollywood establishment', he has worked for a variety of studios (Jaws, E.T. and the Back to the Future films were for Universal, for example, Close Encounters was for Columbia, and indeed virtually saved the studio from bankruptcy, the 'Indiana Jones' trilogy was for Paramount, Poltergeist was for MGM and the two Gremlins films were for Warner Bros). The profits were thus spread fairly evenly throughout the major Hollywood film companies, and helped them all to stay in business. But, he says, 'we must become like Walter Huston in The Treasure of the Sierra Madre – we must put the mountain back'. And few have done more to encourage new talent, whether it be promoting Kathleen Kennedy, Cinderella-style, from student intern and company receptionist to Executive Producer of such films as E.T. and co-founder of Amblin Entertainment or in giving production designer Rick Carter and eight untried directors their first jobs on Steven Spielberg's Amazing Stories for NBC television in the mid-1980s. 'It's like a campus out here,' said Spielberg at the time. 'It's a proving ground, and that's the most exciting part for me. It's really like having a group of film students around, and we're having fun making a project together.'

What is it, then, about Spielberg and his films that creates such popular admiration and such lack of academic, critical and even professional recognition? What is it about his films that, with one or two exceptions, make him the most consistently successful of contemporary filmmakers at the box office? What do his films tell us about him and, perhaps more significantly, what does their appeal tell us about ourselves? And why has his phenomenal success at the box-office hardly been matched by recognition on the part of the industry he has done so much to help keep afloat? These are some of the questions this book will attempt to answer. But I doubt I shall find a better conclusion than that of Martin Amis, who wrote in 1982:

> Filmmakers today – with their target boys and marketing gurus – tie themselves up in knots trying to divine the Lowest Common Denominator of the American public. The rule is: no one ever lost money underestimating the intelligence of the audience. Spielberg doesn't need to do this because in a sense he is there already, uncynically. As an artist, Spielberg is a mirror, not a lamp. His line to the common heart is so direct that he unmans you with the frailty of your own defences, and the transparency of your most intimate fears and hopes.

1

Spielberg: the Man, his Movies and their Meaning

> Creative people in art or architecture or filmmaking or theatre or writing are all products of a collection of impressions from our earlier memories. I don't think there is such a thing as a cathartic flash of white genius light – that's a popular myth. We're all inspired. I'm inspired all the time. But my inspirations are a sum of all my parts and all of my parts started back in 1947 when I was born in Cincinatti, Ohio, and kind of accumulated the dust and pollen of my experiences . . .

Critical reactions to movies are usually more about opinions than they are about facts. First, the facts. Steven Spielberg was born in Cincinnati on 18 December 1947 but was largely raised in Haddonfield, New Jersey, and Scottsdale, Arizona. There, in the heartlands of American suburbia, he cultivated an imagination that would touch the world. He made his first film at the age of 12 in a nondescript suburb of Phoenix and, before he was even 35 years old, he was responsible for directing four of the ten most lucrative films ever made. He was 26 when he started making *Jaws*, 30 when he made *Close Encounters of the Third Kind* and 34 when he made *Raiders of the Lost Ark* with George Lucas. When *E.T. – The Extra Terrestrial* was released in 1982, to become one of the most successful films in box-office history, grossing an astonishing $720,000,000 world-wide ($228.4 million of that in the USA alone, with the total figure still rising well past the billion dollar mark through video sales) he was, at barely 35, the unrivalled 'Peter Pan who would be King of Hollywood' and whose films had reached a degree of social penetration matched by no other filmmaker in history.

Although he is often thought of chiefly as a maker of children's and science fiction films, a reputation consolidated by *Hook*, Spielberg has in fact worked in a variety of film genres, from thrillers (*Duel* [1971] and *The Sugarland Express* [1974]) to horror films (*Jaws* [1975]), comedies (*1941* [1979]) and adventure films (*Raiders of the Lost Ark* [1981], *Indiana Jones and the Temple of Doom* [1984], *Indiana Jones and the Last Crusade* [1989]). And, following an early experiment with *The Color Purple* (1985) and the deeply personal *Empire of the Sun* (1987), he is now beginning to make what are called more 'adult' films, such as the romantic comedy *Always* (1989). Despite this pigeonholing, however, all of Spielberg's films combine elements of comedy, horror, romance, suspense and adventure, not only the ones he has directed but also the ones he has produced (including *Poltergeist* [1982], *Gremlins I* and *II* [1984, 1990] and the three *Back to the Future* films [1985, 1989, 1990]). 'I don't divide my films,' he says; 'it's all just movie-making to me.'

Spielberg does in fact draw a clear distinction between *film*-making and *movie*-making. He defines himself as a movie-maker. His primary intention is to entertain rather than to inform or educate. His detractors are invariably film, rather than movie, critics. Although even they concede that his films are obviously well-made, they dislike what they see as simplistic products, full of special effects, sentimental and almost comic strip in format. They criticize Spielberg for emphasizing the visual and the childlike rather than the substantial or the intellectual. Even in the 13 major films he has directed himself (for, astonishingly, that is all it is at the time of writing) this is a vast overgeneralization. But he has admitted that 'film for me is totally pictorial. I'm more attracted to doing things with pictures and atmospheres – the idea of the visual telling the story.'

That is always his starting point: 'everything is shaped by the story. You don't move the queen without the queen's pawn. I like to tell stories through pictures as opposed to telling them through dialogue.' His skill in doing this is characterized by the sheer pace at which the stories are told. One might think that the stunning visual imagery and special effects so characteristic of his most successful films would be an important means to this end. However, these really only serve as devices for evoking responses that transport the viewer out of his or her reality into an alternative state of mind in which the unbelievable becomes believable and where human emotions become exaggerated and heightened. He has made heavily backlit and slightly diffused lighting effects virtually his own, creating in the process a surrealistic look for many of his films. By pointing light directly into his camera lens, for example Spielberg forces audiences to scrutinize his images more closely and, having thereby pulled them into the story, the light can either bathe the viewer in reassurance or evoke stark fear. 'For me,' he has said, 'movies are busy,

kinetic movement, shadow against light.' His hallmarks are story, lighting, pace and visual and emotional involvement.

The phenomenon of Cinema is a shared experience, individually perceived. As a result, all opinions about it can be said to be equally valid. Certainly, with Spielberg's films, there is rarely room for widely differing individual interpretations concerning what the *story*-lines are in fact about. Their actual *meaning*, however, is something quite different. As a result, Spielberg has had to endure all sorts of weird and wonderful interpretations as to what his work signifies. Robert Kolker, in what is actually the best academic treatment of Spielberg's work, has written:

> Steven Spielberg is the great fantasist of recuperation, every loving son, calling home to find out how things are and assuring the family that everything will be fine. He is the great modern narrator of simple desires fulfilled, of reality diverted into the imaginary spaces of aspirations realized, where fears of abandonment and impotence are turned into fantasy spectacles of security and joyful action . . . security and joy is neither offered by his films nor earned from them, but rather forced upon the viewer, willing or not, by structures that demand complete assent in order to survive. His films are not so much texts to be read and understood, but machines to stimulate desire and fulfill it, to manipulate the viewer without the viewer's awareness of what is happening.

Well, certain individuals might bring greater experience, greater know-ledge or greater sensitivity to their observations but the fact remains that appreciation, or lack of it, is shaped by the degree to which the director has been successful in communicating his vision to his audience via his art form. And Hollywood movie-makers have proved more successful than any other nation's body of film directors in appealing to audiences not just within their own society, but worldwide. Film scholars have summarized years of research into this phenomenon by labelling it the 'Classic Hollywood Style'.

During the 1920s, when Hollywood was conquering the world's cinema screens, American films attracted non-American audiences

Steven Spielberg (*right*) and George Lucas (*left*) on the set of *Raiders of the Lost Ark*, 1981, a Lucasfilm Ltd production. Directed by Spielberg and produced by Frank Marshall the screenplay was based on a story by George Lucas and Philip Kaufman. Together with its sequels, the 'Lucasberger' formula was to see a return to the style of the 1930s and 1940s action-adventure films that had done so much to thrill them as boys combined with state-of-the-art special effects that they have made their own.

because they seemed to offer the very things they saw as quintessentially American: pace, movement, progress, optimism, lavishness, sentimentality. It is no accident that Spielberg's films are still doing that. 'I always consider the international market when I make a film,' he said following the release of *Close Encounters*, recognizing the differences in approaches to cinema on either side of the Atlantic:

> It was obvious to me that I would discuss the film more overseas than in the US. In the US, I merely discussed the flashiness and the sound, the excitement, the phenomena. Here in Europe I am discussing the story and the philosophy; the symbolism.

But just in case Spielberg's 'non-intellectual' mask should slip too far, he is quick to state that 'there comes a point when you have to forget the audience and try to please yourself.' For him, that point arrives once filming actually begins, but by that time he has already done most of his forward planning and preparation.

Audiences are not normally aware of the kind of work that goes into a film, from the idea stage to final edit; mostly they are concerned simply with whether the final product has pleased them. Spielberg's success in doing this is partly attributable to the fact that during the planning stages he gets his early thinking about films that will satisfy audiences, that *he* would want to see, instinctively right. Once the filming starts, it is a logistical, technical and creative exercise that needs to be conducted without worrying about possible audience reactions. By relying on his instincts, he makes a very complicated business look easy.

Spielberg, as we have seen, is far more successful in communicating with audiences than he is with critics. Whereas audiences enter a movie theatre to be entertained, critics enter it to be impressed. The former operate on the assumption that they have paid to see an individual product and judge it accordingly in absolute terms, whereas the latter is invited to judge it relative to a whole host of broader comparative references – previous performances of crew and cast, how the film relates to the book, and so on. Such people bring the baggage of the outside world inside the darkened auditorium and look for points of identification regardless of what the filmmaker is trying to say. When, for example, he was criticized for 'Spielbergizing' Alice Walker's novel *The Color Purple*, Spielberg rightly said that those who claimed he had turned the book into a sentimentalist, racist, or sexist tract merely demonstrated 'the limitations of people who write about movies. They're separate from those who go to them. They [audiences] look at *The Color Purple* for what it is. They don't link it up analytically with anything I've done before.'

It is, however, possible to analyse certain common elements running through all Spielberg's films that provide them with their consistent appeal. It might appear at first glance that they are indeed essentially simple stories, simply told. True, they are mostly straightforward narratives, but they are told in such a way as to affect us all, both as individuals *and* as an audience. Given that Spielberg's concern is primarily twofold, namely to entertain and to trigger mass emotion, his success in doing both in film after film does beg understanding. When our emotions can be so readily manipulated, cinema can tell us something about ourselves.

Spielberg's films appeal to common emotions that most of us can understand, either because we relate to them now or because we can remember a time when we would have been more directly affected by them. We can accept or reject the validity of the path that Spielberg chooses to take us along, but the people who follow his lead clearly enjoy being manipulated by him. Hence Spielberg's preoccupation with childhood and adolescence, with innocence before the fall into adulthood, and with nostalgia, would appear to reflect preoccupations within us all. His films offer illusions of what once was and, for a couple of hours at least, of what still is and what still might be. Their sheer humanity strips away socially manufactured veneers of disillusionment and cynicism and reminds us of our inner selves before the real world got to us – which is why we started going to the movies in the first place.

This might all seem fanciful gobbledegook. Perhaps we should simply see the films as telling stories in a way that all human beings can understand. This is because their form and structure falls within an established pattern of classical story-telling that is easily identifiable and accessible as a cultural product we can all relate to. We have sampled the product before by watching films made in the classical Hollywood style and just when we stopped buying cinema tickets because the product was no longer satisfying, along comes a filmmaker who does provide us with what we really want because that is what we feel most comfortable with. His films do not after all confront us with difficult or unpalatable issues that require painful or agonizing moral decisions. They ask us merely to escape for a few hours into a world (or indeed into a universe) in which, despite its often fantastic subject matter, we can believe in and enjoy.

Or do they? At their most basic level, Spielberg's films certainly appeal to the child in everyone. The young and the young at heart revel in their capacity to reinforce that aspect of their personality. In swimming pools and on beaches all around the world, for example, children of all ages still mimic the sounds and actions of the shark in *Jaws*. *E.T.* helped the Kuwahara dirt bicycle to become top of every child's Christmas present list, and the instantly recognizable 'Sky Tones' of *Close Encounters* can still be heard on countless doorbells the world over. There is nothing new in the intensive marketing of products that has accompanied many of his films; Walt Disney had long before established the pattern of marketing devices with a certain cartoon mouse, and, like Disney, images Spielberg has created have helped to forge the collective vision of the planet's increasingly global culture.

But it is not just his ability to create universal fads that merits attention; just as film is far too serious a business to be left to the critics, neither can it be judged by reference to the marketing gurus. Spielberg's films have in fact helped to shape the perceptions of an entire generation of filmgoers, from the final stages of the Vietnam conflict in the mid 1970s to Ronald Reagan's America of the 1980s, although more perhaps in cultural than in political terms.

The 'first defeat in American military history' scarred the national psyche. The experience of the first televised war, in the period from the assassination of President Kennedy in 1963 to the humiliating evacuation of Saigon in 1975, was one that most Americans preferred to forget. Having seen the war fought and lost on their television sets, they certainly did not want to see it on their cinema screens. It would be some time before the nation was ready to tackle the trauma of Vietnam, for now it wanted escapist or fantasy films. In 1977, having had to endure national humiliation, assassinations, Watergate and the presidencies of Gerald Ford and Jimmy Carter, many would have liked to have gone aboard the alien spaceship of *Close Encounters of the Third Kind* along with Richard Dreyfuss. Hollywood helped to begin the process of recuperation through acceptance with such films as *The Deer Hunter* (1978) and *Apocalypse Now!* (1979), although films dealing with the alienation of the individual from society reflected the 1970s ideological climate of disillusionment – *Dirty Harry* (1971) and *Taxi Driver* (1976), for example. Then came the difficulties faced by returning Vietnam veterans rejected by the society for which they had fought but lost, as in *Coming Home* (1978). The 1970s ended with the Iranian Revolution and the seizure of the American hostages in Tehran and with growing Soviet muscle-flexing, culminating in the invasion of Afghanistan. Accordingly, when Ronald Reagan became President in 1980 on the day the hostages came home, it appeared to many that the time had at last come to return 'home' to the past of American greatness, to rebuild society from the very source of its historic strength: the American family home. If it took someone who understood images as well as an ageing Hollywood movie star to revitalize the myth, then so be it. The fusion of image and reality had found its Oppenheimer.

While the Reagan Administration sought to create days of future past on the political front, Hollywood in the meantime had discovered a filmmaker who could provide an escape back to the future on the cultural

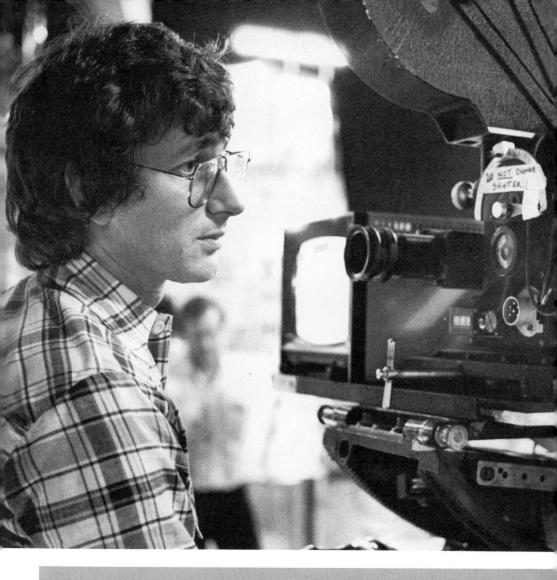

Spielberg directing in 1977. His boyish looks, even at age 30, unfairly earned him a 'Movie Brat' label but he was to help inspire a whole new generation of young film-makers who dominated American movie-making in the 1980s.

front. Spielberg didn't realize it, but his preoccupation with his own childhood and his own fall from innocence was about to become a national syndrome. Yet ironically, the man who was to emerge in the 1970s and 1980s as America's most popular film director and producer was able to achieve this stature by being largely unaffected – at least not directly – by the events that agitated his generation so much. 'I grew up in the 60s,' he said, 'but I was never into flower power, or Vietnam protests, like all my friends. I was always at the movies.'

This perhaps provides a clue to his ability to supply his and other generations with the movies that they can use to escape from their worries. It is almost as if he was saying: 'If you had gone to the movies like I did then you wouldn't have been so worked up about those nasty events but, as you are so angst-ridden, here is an example of the kind of movies that I used to watch for entertainment and escape which might help you now.' But if therein lies the key to the popularity of his films in America, it was not because Spielberg was consciously aware of his uncanny ability to anticipate audience desires:

> I've always made the kinds of films that I, as an audience, would want to see. That's been my main philosophy. I've never been a social thinker in my cineaste life. In my personal life, very much so. But I've never been one to say, 'I think this picture is going to change the way America thinks' . . . I feel that if I found a subject that would be beneficial for everyone to see, I would probably do it for television because that medium reaches more households than motion pictures ever can. I mean, my goodness, *E.T.* is the biggest film of all time around the world but the same number of people see two episodes of 'Cosby' over two weeks as have seen *E.T.* in the United States.

That said, however, films are mirrors of society as well as products of their times and their appeal does reflect the psychology of the audiences going to see them. They are cultural products, invested with an ideology not always immediately apparent – even to the director. Again avoiding anything like an intellectual approach, he has said: 'All the films had personal cores, and that's really what I look for when I look to make a movie. But they have been, as I've heard people say, high in concept – whatever that means – sounds great; high concept, you can't fail with a high concept.'

Although here we are primarily concerned with what Spielberg himself was trying to say through his films, his influence over film-making in the America of the 1980s, not only as a director but also as a producer, is such that one can almost discern a school of American filmmaking (including George Lucas, Robert Zemeckis, Don Bluth and Joe Dante). Their success at the box-office would suggest a cultural phenomenon the ideology of which requires interpretation. Even Spielberg himself has admitted:

> So, yes, there are national mood swings. There are times when people want sex and violence in films. And there are times when people crave innocence, a return to their childhoods. But, as a filmmaker, you can't ride

with that. You've got to ride with your own feelings at any time and hope people respond.

Well, maybe so, but it is Spielberg's ability to make his own feelings *correspond and coincide* to those national mood swings that rests at the heart of his success and appeal – and of his significance.

This is not done by making films with overtly political themes. Where such themes are appropriate to the story, Spielberg deliberately plays them down, which in turn is part of his technique of underinforming his audiences on certain narrative issues:

> I believe in not giving the audience what they want, because their collective imagination is much greater than mine. That was why in *Jaws* I decided to leave the 'Enemy of the People' part of the story not that well told. I felt the same way about *Close Encounters*. The military cover-up, for example, I didn't want to beat to death because in the US it's passé. We have lived through Watergate, the CIA, and people already find them redundant.

This understatement is a major reason why his films are so typically American. They fuel the American dream in which audiences just want to play, party and fantasize and as such they exploit the quest for life, liberty and the pursuit of happiness.

In Spielberg's universe, audiences tend to know where they stand. His films are adventure playgrounds with all the joys and hazards, the certainties and the uncertainties, associated with play. We know, for example, that there are dangerous sharks under the water or mad truck drivers on the roads and we suspect that there might be life on other planets or life after death. Younger audiences revel in the reinforcement of their childlike fantasies, while adults are reminded of how they once saw that world, and are taken back there. Spielberg's skill is in confronting us with a world that we as adults might well have thought we had lost but that he returns us to by playing on our sense of common experience. For children, it is the universe as it is; for adults, who think they know better, it is the universe as it should have been. Because we all remember childhood fears and fantasies, we can relate directly to this known playground, this shared nostalgia, draw comfort from it, and revel in its reappearance on film. Spielberg has said that 'I was a kid in a sandbox with a lot of toys for many, many years as a film-maker' – the important thing is that he is rare amongst children in that he lets other kids play with his toys.

His stories are always, none the less, rooted firmly in our known universe, playing on our fears of it while stretching our imagination into areas that reinforce the values of childhood. Spielberg helps us escape into fantasy by providing us with a comfortable universe in which we know good will triumph over evil and where we know that all will come right in the end. There are, of course, uncomfortable moments along the way, but our knowledge that goodness will prevail provides us with a reassurance and comfort that will enable us to endure any of the difficulties and sticky moments that he throws at us.

This observation has led certain analysts to conclude that Spielberg's films are ideologically conservative: Robert Kolker for example:

> 'the form and structure of the films produce images and narratives that respond or give shape to the current ideological needs of an audience, offering a safe and secure ideological haven . . . The films offer nothing new beyond their spectacle, nothing the viewer does not already want, does not immediately accept. That is their conservative power, and it has spread thought the cinema of the eighties.'

Although it is not quite fair to say that the films offer nothing new beyond their spectacle, this is an interesting observation. On the simplest level, it is true that his films usually introduce us to characters who are basically ordinary people much like ourselves. By placing ordinary people in extraordinary situations he poses questions such as: 'How would *you* shape up to confronting a Great White Shark while out swimming?'; 'Would *you* go aboard a gigantic alien mothership if one arrived here?'; 'Would *you* stare into the Ark of the Covenant out of curiosity if after a biblical upbringing you knew what its consequences might be?'; 'Would *you* hide a squidgy alien in your bedroom and would you ask for adult support if you knew it was dying?'; 'Would *you* relinquish your one true love to a rival suitor if you were killed in an accident and came back as a ghost?' He achieves this simply by placing himself in the same situation and asking: 'What would *I* do?' These may not be profound issues, but they are great fun. The identification process between audience and screen character is a key element in his success:

> Each of my movies has showed enough humanity to allow the audience to identify with the person who is having the experience. I haven't made my *It's a Wonderful Life* [Frank Capra's 1946 ghost story that features on the TV set throughout *Gremlins*] . . . I will someday. But in the meantime I wouldn't be satisfied with my films if there weren't human beings functioning as your guide through this world of mechanized madness.

Almost accidentally, Spielberg's determination to use immediately identifiable characters has led to the discovery of the value of not always using big stars in his films so as not to detract from the audience's ability to relate easily to the situations he presents. When asked about his philosophy of good drama, Spielberg replied in the following terms:

> For me, it's someone – a protagonist – who is no longer in control of his life, who loses control and then has to somehow regain it. That's good drama. All of my pictures have had external forces working on the protagonist. In almost every Hitchcock film, the protagonist loses control early in the first act. Then he not only has to get it back, he has to address the situation. That theme has followed me through my films, too.

Spielberg believes that Richard Dreyfuss, who he has used as a central character in three of his films, is 'as close an actor to Spencer Tracy as exists today . . . he represents the underdog in all of us.'

> He is a lot like Everyman at the same time. Richard's easier to identify with than, say, Robert Redford. Most of us are like Richard Dreyfuss. Few of us are like Bob Redford or Steve McQueen. I've always believed in the movies I've made, my central protagonist has always been – and probably always will be – Mr Everyday Regular Fella.

Spielberg therefore is really using this identification to prepare us for the extraordinary events that his characters – that we – are about to experience. Dreyfuss has said of Spielberg that he 'has a love affair going with the suburban middle class' and this group perhaps constitutes Spielberg's main audience although his films also appeal to young people from poorer backgrounds. This is a narrative device that enables him to lure us into what appears to be a false sense of security so that we can be thrilled or shocked by what is to follow. 'The play's the thing,' he said in 1982. 'In every movie I have made, the movie is the star.' He did claim later that he had no objections to utilizing stars – even wanting Robert Redford and Paul Newman to play the leads in *Always* when he first thought about making the film about ten years previously, and of course Harrison Ford and Sean Connery were huge stars by the time they appeared in *Indiana Jones and the Last Crusade* – but his films generally have benefited enormously from not having stars for audiences to ogle to the detriment of the story. Perhaps he learned from the early experience of *The Sugarland Express*, when people went expecting to see a particular kind of film because it starred the popular comedienne Goldie Hawn (who none the less gave a fine dramatic performance). More recently, however, he has shown with *Hook* that he is now prepared to exploit the 'stars' by casting the likes of Dustin Hoffman, Robin Williams and Julia Roberts in his updating of the Peter Pan story.

The key perhaps lies in Spielberg's statement that 'I want to make reality something fun to live with because that is what it is. I don't want people to escape from reality – but to escape *with* reality'. 'Making movies is an illusion, a technical illusion that people fall for,' he said in 1978. 'My job is to take that technique and hide it so well that never once are you taken out of your chair and reminded of where you are.' Spielberg thus provides us with a temporary escape into a world we already know. And the popularity of his films could perhaps be interpreted as a reflection of the inherent desire of the ultimately conservative audiences to 'play it safe,' to dabble in escapism without any of the risks. But one thing is clear. Spielberg is not prepared to provide all the answers to questions posed by his storylines:

> I don't think in any of my films the end answers all the questions. I think in everything I've done . . . each act has a climax so that the final act probably answers the most cosmic question but not everything. Why? Why spoon-feed? Why set out a buffet? So the audience can walk out of the theatre knowing more than they did coming in?

The sheer pace of Spielberg's films seduces the audience into suspending its critical faculties. This is done largely by playing upon emotional reactions within us all, which enables various anomalies within the storylines to be overlooked. How, for example, does Indiana Jones' girlfriend in *Raiders of the Lost Ark* escape from the exploding truck? How does Indy himself in the same film actually get inside the Nazi submarine? Why can't E.T. heal himself in the same way he can Elliot's cuts and bruises and revive pot plants? And given that their destinies had merged into one, why didn't Elliott die when E.T. did? Spielberg's early television training was crucial in his development of narrative pace, because of that medium's need to deliver its goods in accordance within strict dramatic and scheduling limits. Television, in other words, taught Spielberg how to stay several steps ahead of the audience and thereby prevent boredom creeping in.

This does not mean, however, that he is unwilling to provide a clue-ridden map rather like the one followed by the children in his production of *The Goonies* (1985):

> I think that most of the movies I've made have been movies where a journey is involved. The goal is always in sight in the first act. A lot of my films are question-answer pictures leading up to an inevitable conclusion that the audience is waiting for, and hopefully they won't be disappointed. I think every movie I've made promises an arrival zone, and it's just the kind of drama that intrigues me.

During the making of *Close Encounters*, a film that ends with an 'arrival zone' that is really a point of departure, Spielberg discovered that several government departments were worried that it might cause panic reminiscent of that caused by Orson Welles' famous 1938 radio broadcast of 'War of the Worlds', which preyed on invasion fears. Spielberg said:

> Today it's just the opposite. I knew that if this film was to be popular it wouldn't be because people were afraid of the phenomena, but because the UFOs are a seductive alternative for a lot of people who no longer have faith in anything.

Because his films undoubtedly tap the mood of their audiences, Spielberg has emerged almost accidentally as a spokesman of his generation. This has prompted one of the more sensible analysts to write that: 'Spielberg's films constitute a factory of ideological production, the great imagery of the eighties, full of images the culture wanted to see. The frequency, success, and influence of his films during a relatively short period of time have made them a kind of encyclopaedia of desire, a locus of representations to which audiences wished to be called.' Although Spielberg does not particularly welcome this heady responsibility, stating in 1978 that 'I'm not really that preoccupied with being the spokesman for the paranoid seventies, because I'm not really that paranoid in real life', his films none the less have provided audiences with opportunities to tackle their own hopes and fears. And, when one considers the themes of *Duel* and *Jaws*, not to mention *Poltergeist* and elements of *Close Encounters* and *E.T.*, it is impossible to conclude otherwise than that Spielberg is indeed fascinated by paranoia as a human condition.

As long ago as 1978, after less than a handful of films, Spielberg commented:

> People have drawn the conclusion that because most of my films are about concepts, I make concept movies – as opposed to films where the story starts with the individual's emotional problems and blossoms from there. The story [supposedly] starts with a broader concept, and the people join the concept. The concept is the engine, and the people are the coal tender. Because most of my pictures *aren't* concept-oriented, it isn't necessarily the case that they haven't grown out of personal dilemmas or my own personal centre.

This final point is crucial to an understanding of Spielberg's work. With the notable exception of the early and carefully calculated short film *Amblin'*(1969), which was designed specifically to get him noticed by the movie industry, each of his films is a sort of mini-autobiography, invested with all sorts of clues as to the man's view of himself, of the world around him, of his past and his hopes for the future.

Commenting on the success of his three most successful films, *Jaws, Close Encounters* and *E.T.*, Spielberg has said:

> I can't tell you why they were so successful. I've never set out to coincide with audience tastes or moods. I make what I want to make. I've never 'crystal-balled' a fad. If *Jaws* had been made three years earlier, it would still have been a hit. *E.T.* could have been made four years either side of Ronald Reagan, although it wouldn't have done as well in the early '70s and I don't think it would do so well in the 1990s.

Spielberg's ability to create cinematic blackholes into which the audience is irresistibly drawn, destroying the viewers' emotional defences in the process, is almost mechanical in its efficiency. If his films are indeed machines, then Spielberg is the engine. Even his so-called 'flops' – *1941* and *Empire of the Sun* being the most often cited – were not sufficiently disastrous to alienate his audiences. But, he believes, there has been a price to pay because

> in a way I have been typecast – by audiences even, not just by critics – and in a way that gives me less of a chance to make a sleeper or to break through with something that's very unusual for me to tackle. But I'm still going to try to do that. I'm not going to cater just to being expensive or lavish [or making] adventure movies or science-fiction movies.

Even when he attempted to break free with *The Color Purple*, he revealed himself to be first and foremost a story-teller in the finest classical tradition. His passionate desire to spin a yarn cinematographically, to tell a story combining moving images and words as a means of invoking the full range of human emotions, surpasses all other motivations.

It might be tempting to see Spielberg's development in linear terms; once the boy grew up to be a man – which took some time (around his late 30s) – his preoccupation changed to more adult themes, with *Always* for example being his first real attempt to tackle a heterosexual love story between adults. Again, this would be too simple an approach. He himself said in 1990:

> I've been thinking a lot about a certain thing which is, essentially, that we are who we are every year. Every year we change – I hope we change every year. I hope we don't stay exactly the same and the movies are simply a reflection of who you happen to be on that particular month when that film is released or the year that it took to write and create the story and the movie.

Always, 1989, was Spielberg's first real attempt to tackle a heterosexual love story between adults.

The following year would reveal that Spielberg, through Robin Williams, was still Peter Pan.

Spielberg is more than happy to discuss his aspirations and intentions in just about every area – with the exception (quite rightly) of his private life. 'Personally,' he said in 1985, 'I have always learned a lot about myself from my films. If there is a darker side to me, then it will come out in one of them. They are almost cathartic for me.' In 1978, after only three American cinema releases, two of which are still in the top 10 films of all time, he said:

> I'm still fighting so I can be good in my eyes. When I'm good in my eyes I might even quit. I don't see that happening for years. I haven't satisfied myself with a film yet. I haven't made a film that I think is great. *Jaws*, *Sugarland Express* and *Close Encounters of the Third Kind* are not the films I could have made five years from now and hopefully as you get deeper in life and deeper in values . . . as I find myself caring more for people, the people around me, the people whom I love, my family, I find

my films get much more personal, much more emotional, and I think that I'll be a good film-maker when I eventually can make that turn and deal with that material and start with a personal problem and let the personal problem create the excitement.

Nevertheless, even his early films contain so many autobiographical touches that it is possible through them to ascertain a great deal about how Spielberg saw himself at the time he made any given movie and thus to build up a picture of the man through his movies.

Take, for example, the yearning-for-home theme so evident in many of his films. This is as near to being autobiographical as it is possible to get, from *The Sugarland Express* in 1974, in which a desperate couple try desperate measures to restore their child back to the heart of the nuclear family, to the more recent *Always*, a ghost story where 'home' is life itself. In between, *E.T.* 'phoned home', Robert Shaw sang 'Show Me the Way to Go Home' in *Jaws*, seized humans are returned home by the Mothership in *Close Encounters*, Nettie is separated from her sister's home in *The Color Purple*, and Jim is caught up in his wartorn home of Shanghai in *Empire of the Sun*.

> I think the longing for home comes from my own life. I've lived in so many places since I was a child I felt I never really had a home, and that's a feeling many people can respond to.

His own experience therefore exploits audience memories and fears, playing upon the childlike desire to return to the safety and comfort of the family home where all the unpleasant things associated with adulthood – like laundry and tidying up – are taken care of for you. This enables the audience to concentrate on fantasies, and Spielberg's films recreate many of those fantasies as a form of entertainment - but also as a form of escape. This is because, at least until he discovered the escapist value of fantasy, Spielberg's own childhood was not particularly happy (he described it as 'semi-unhappy'), due mainly to having to move house so often and to his parents constantly rowing. This meant illicitly watching television ('I was, and still am, a TV junkie,' he said in 1986), going to the movies and, finally by the age of twelve, actually making his own films.

As a very young child growing up in the 1950s at the start of America's golden television age, the young Steven was not allowed to watch just anything on television. He was quite simply terrified by a great deal of what was on; he remembers particularly a documentary on snakes that made him cry – the genesis of Indiana Jones's greatest fear? Television provided him not so much with a window on the world as with a mirror into his own imagination. But like the Jones character who had to overcome his phobia in order to perform superhuman feats, Steven likewise found himself being compelled back to the television set:

I liked being scared. It was very stimulating. In my films I celebrate the imagination as a tool of great creation and a device for the ultimate scream, and even as a kid I liked pushing myself to the brink of terror and then pulling back. In the morning I was the bravest guy – little seven year old Steven walking around the closet or talking to the trees, saying 'I'm not afraid of you'.

Fear, and his efforts to overcome it, is in fact something that permeates a great deal of Spielberg's persona – despite his parents' efforts to protect him from the fearful influence of television, let alone their disintegrating relationship. 'My parents did strictly guard the tube from my impressionable eyes.' His father used to set a trap to monitor his viewing by placing a hair over the on-switch, but 'I always found the hair, memorized its position, and replaced it when I was through.' Apart from the odd sneak illicit viewing of *Dragnet*, more usually 'television to me was Imogene Coca, Sid Caesar [whom Spielberg was to hire for one of his *Amazing Stories* in later life], Soupy Sales and *The Honeymooners*.' Denied

Audrey Hepburn makes a special appearance as Hap, the spiritual guide who sends Pete back to earth to complete his mission, in *Always*.

'official' access to the decade's better TV programmes, and with television in Arizona anyway ending for him at 10.30pm ('we had nothing, except probably the worst television you've ever seen'), he was raised on a diet of *The Mickey Mouse Club* or Mickey Rooney in *The Atomic Kid* ('I knew Mickey Rooney really well at the end of my stay in Phoenix').

As for the cinema, he went when his over-protective parents allowed him to go. He was not one of those kids who hung around cinemas or who always frequented the Saturday morning matinee. He had to make do with films either his parents wanted to see (such as Audrey Hepburn in *Funny Face* [1957]; he was to employ her as an angel in *Always* over 20 years later) or with films they thought he should see (such as Danny Kaye in *The Court Jester* [1956]) or with films they thought he would like to see (such as Disney cartoons and adventures). It was only later, when the family moved to California, that he had access to the art house circuit and the works of the great directors of the sound era, such as Antonioni, Bergman, Godard, Kurosawa, Resnais, Tati, Truffaut: 'anything that wasn't American impressed me'. This influence has been seen in his use of montage and in many experimental techniques employed in his early television and film work. When he did come belatedly to appreciate Hollywood directors, he was thus better equipped to cast a discerning eye over their work and draw from their strengths. He did not, for example, 'think that Preston Sturges was so amazing with his camera, but he made some of the greatest movies ever made':

> And I don't think Howard Hawks was as visionary and audacious as John Ford with the camera, and yet Hawks made some films that were better than some of the films Ford made. I don't think there is such a thing as a bad director, but there *are* bad story-tellers.

Or, as he said elsewhere:

> I admire directors like Michael Curtiz and Victor Fleming, who are the unsung heroes and the workhorses of the '30s and '40s. They were upstaged by great film-makers like Hitchcock and Capra and Sturges, who had their own personal signatures. These directors didn't have signatures; they were chameleons. They could adapt to any story, in any period, with any premise.

It was thus his sensitivity to a good story, well told, which first attracted him to the media of film and television, and which has motivated him ever since.

The first film he remembers seeing was Cecil B. De Mille's *The Greatest Show on Earth* (presumably when he was about four or five since the film was released in 1952).

Spielberg, who produced MGM's science-horror story *Poltergeist*, 1982, with Frank Marshall, is seen on the set with director Tobe Hooper and Craig T. Nelson who stars.

My father said: 'It's going to be bigger than you but that's alright. The people in it are going to be up on a screen and they can't get out at you.' But there they *were* up on that screen and *they were getting out at me*. I guess ever since then I've wanted to try to involve the audience as much as I can, so that they no longer think they're sitting in an audience.

Later in life, he again talked about his early movie theatre experiences and their impact upon him: 'The first three movies I ever saw were all Walt Disney films, and they scared the bejeezus out of me, and I was absolutely apoplectic with fear when I got home at six or seven years old.' During *Snow White and the Seven Dwarfs*, for example, 'when the wicked queen turned into a hag and a skeleton crumbled into pieces, I burst into tears and started shaking. For three or four nights I had to crawl into bed with my mom and dad.'

Even at home there was no escape from the terrifying things that appeared on the television, despite his parents miscalculations as to what would or would not frighten him. As an adult, he was able to parody the supposedly evil impact of television in Tobe Hooper's *Poltergeist* in 1982, which he produced but also supervised closely from original story to final cut, and which he described as 'my revenge on TV'. Not only does he have the television switched on virtually all the time even now, but he also has one starring in most of his films.

Spielberg's desire to get into the entertainment industry, he explained, was 'part of that whole deprivation thing [which] I think inspired me to get into the business that I was denied when I was young.' When he did manage to break into the industry, television was his first port of call. He was thrown into the deep end by Universal Studios when NBC told him to direct the formidable Joan Crawford in an episode of Rod Serling's *Night Gallery* called 'Eyes'. It is perhaps ironic that a man who was later to avoid using big stars in his movie career, began by directing one of Hollywood's most glittering stars in her television debut. Spielberg said that the project was simply something 'that was assigned to me . . . on the basis of 'You've just turned 21. You want to be a professional director? Here's a show. Go, direct it.' One apocryphal story has it that Crawford refused to be seen in public with him in case she was taken for his mother. He said of her: 'She's a very nice woman – the only person on the crew who treated me like I had been working 50 years . . . she understood that I shouldn't have been making that particular show: I should have been making something out of my imagination.' Elsewhere, he has said:

> She was terrific, totally professional. She relied on me to direct her more than I ever thought she would. When I first met her, I thought she was going to tell me how to direct her. In fact, she kept coming up to me asking one question after another about her character and what she should be doing. I was prepared to answer some of her questions, but not all of them. She expected me to be George Cukor and I never thought that she would lend herself to me totally, and on my first time out.

He confessed to finding the prospect of such responsibility with only the experience of his teenage films behind him as being 'a very traumatic experience'. He did his best to combat his fears, concentrating on the project 'more like a menu of shots, a memorandum of things to do each day' rather than on the overall story. Watching him making himself ill with worry, Crawford's co-star, Barry Sullivan, took him to one side and told him 'Life is short. Don't put yourself through this if you don't have to.'

But he did have to. Driven by his burning ambition, yet tied to a seven-year contract he was already beginning to regret, there was nothing else to do except bite the bullet and work out his professional apprenticeship as he went on to direct almost a dozen episodes for various TV series such as (in chronological order) *Marcus Welby M.D.*, *The Psychiatrists*, *The Name of the Game*, and *Owen Marshall*, as well as the opening episode of the first *Colombo* series, entitled 'Murder by the Book'. Of this 'routine assignment work', only two comparatively enjoyable experiences stood out for him. The *Colombo* episode was 'fun' because it was 'mostly watching'; although Peter Falk had already made two television pilot movies with the character, Spielberg's was the first of the series, 'and Peter was still finding things. I was able to discover 'Columbo-isms' along with Peter that he's [since] kept in his repertoire.' He felt, however, that his best early television work with actors was on *The Psychiatrists*, for which he directed two episodes, and which proved 'very interesting' because he was able 'to cause input in the writing of it . . . So it was a real challenge.' The producer of the series, Jerry Friedman,

> had his own longhair film society right in the heart of Universal Studios. He employed a number of writers, directors, people dealing with esoterica, and he hired people from his college and people he knew from the East. I was just a young person, whom he liked at the time, and to whom he said, 'Here, do two *Psychiatrists* for me.'

The first episode was tailor-made for Spielberg, being a story about a six-year-old boy 'lost in the world of fantasy and comic books'. The second, which he filmed back-to-back with the first, concerned a dying top golf professional (played by Clu Galager) whose friends present him in hospital with the dirt and grass and flag of their local golf course's 18th hole.

> Clu began to cry – as a person and as an actor. His immediate response when the camera was rolling was to burst into tears. He tore the grass out of the hole and he squeezed the dirt all over himself and he thanked them for bringing him this gift, the greatest gift he had ever received. It was just a very moving moment that came out of being loose with an idea. Everything didn't have to be locked down because of so many hours in the day and so much film in the camera and so much money in the budget. You could do more things like that and make a film grow and make characters come to life more.

Despite his meticulous advance planning and 'storyboarding', Spielberg is more than happy to improvise with actors once filming begins. 'I storyboard everything, and maybe that relates to Disney. Most directors don't, of course. I do all the preliminary sketches myself and then hire a sketch artist to do them in detail. We work it out shot by shot.' Nor does such preparation make him immovable when it comes to setting up shots:

> Where I put the camera is something I do intuitively. I don't think I do a lot of planning. My storyboards are in no way about actual camera angles or about what kind of lens I should employ. They only show me what I need to do to get across the story points of a scene.

The authors of the *Columbo* episode, William Link and Barry Levinson (the latter of whom directed *Young Sherlock Holmes* for Spielberg in 1986, and won the Oscar for *Rain Man* in 1989) also wrote Spielberg's third television movie, *Savage*, a private eye-cum-investigative reporter tale. Levinson spoke highly of 'natural' directorial skills from 'the kid they said didn't know people', whereas Link described Spielberg's early television work as 'dazzling, electrifying . . . He took all sorts of chances. He'd do a five-page scene in one take, choreographing the people and the camera.' 'TV,' said Spielberg years later, 'taught me to think on my feet. You have six days to shoot 50 pages of script. TV is a well-oiled machine. Either you roll with it or it rolls over you.'

Television thus helped Spielberg to cut his teeth in the entertainment business. It also helped to bring his story-telling skills to the notice of Hollywood with a television movie that was so successful it was released on the big screen as a feature in Europe. This was *Duel*, a 75-minute story of an ordinary American suburbanite who is inexplicably menaced by a truck whose driver is never identified. The programme attracted a little attention in America but when an extended version was shown at the Cannes Film Festival, that doyenne of British film critics, Dilys Powell, was so impressed with it that she rounded up other judges and made them watch it. Following her rave review in the *Sunday Times*, the film went on general release throughout Europe, where it did steady business and built up a cult following. The irony of Spielberg, the admirer of British films, being 'discovered' by an English film critic was not lost on him: 'if it weren't for your illustrious predecessor,' he told Iain Johnstone in 1984, 'I don't think I'd be here today.'

Two more television films followed *Duel*. In 1972, Spielberg made *Something Evil*, a horror movie about a. New York family who buy a haunted country house only to find their children become the victims of demonic possession. There are many Hitchcockian touches evident and the film anticipated the success of *The Exorcist* (1973), Robert Klaus' screenplay for Spielberg having already been written before William Friedkin's film was made. Two particular aspects of this project fore-shadowed Spielberg's future success. First, there was the extraordinary performance of the boy, played by Johnny Whittaker, who was known for playing sweetness and delight in *Family Affair*. Spielberg demonstrated his talent for extracting outstanding performances from young people. Then there was his creation of extraordinary lighting effects: 'light is like a magnet – it can veil something wondrous or, as in the flashlights on *E.T.*, something terrifying. The first scary thing I learned to do as a child was turn off the light!' In *Something Evil*

> It was the first time in a television film that hot windows were used; those were all sets and 'burned up' all the windows to give a hellish effect outside . . . anytime anyone passes by a window, they almost disappear because the window is so bright they fade out and become stick figures until they pass beyond the light. I thought that the house should be surrounded by a wholly white hell-heat and it worked very well.

It was also during this project, in which he made one of his rare, if brief and reluctant screen appearances, that Spielberg discovered the talents of cinematographer Bill Butler and actor-writer Carl Gottleib – both of whom he would employ a few years later on his major breakthrough project, *Jaws*.

In light of the overseas success of *Duel* in 1973, Universal decided to promote him to the big screen with *The Sugarland Express* (1974). Powell's American counterpart, Pauline Kael, reviewed *Sugarland* in the *New Yorker*, stating that 'in terms of the pleasure that technical assurance gives an audience, this film is one of the most phenomenal directoral debuts in the history of the movies' and compared him to Howard Hawks. Although she was not to prove quite so effusive about his later films, it was a tremendous boost to the start of his film career and he was hailed (inaccurately) by others as the latest addition to the new generation of film school educated 'Movie Brats'. Not all had the talent to survive. But, like Francis Ford Coppola (UCLA), Brian De Palma (NYU) and George Lucas (USC), Steven Spielberg did.

After he had established himself on the big screen, which he was able to do thanks to television, he was to return to the small screen in the mid-eighties with his anthology series, *Amazing Stories*. This in turn enabled him to put on screen many of his childhood stories and fantasies, and the series has many echoes of those programmes that Steven was forbidden to see as a boy, such as *The Twilight Zone* and *The Outer Limits*. Many episodes are based upon Spielberg-inspired bedtime stories, although not all are as strong as they could be. 'I get too many ideas,' he said in 1985, 'and I want to act on them all. *Amazing Stories* is a foster home for ideas that will never grow into adulthood, that aren't strong enough to stretch beyond 23 minutes.' By the mid-eighties, of course, Spielberg had become a leading figure in the group of producer-directors who were able to make just about any movie they wanted. But Spielberg is unusual in that he does not see the distinction normally drawn by filmmakers between television and cinema; the screen is bigger in one and you can have impressive special effects on it, but it is the story that really counts. *E.T.*, with only about 30 special effects, proves that. And as he himself has said, 'I've just grown up with TV, as all of us have, and there is a lot of television inside my brain that I wish I could get out of there. You can't help it – once it's in there, it's like a tattoo.'

His love of television is matched only by his love of movies, especially once he had been exposed to Walt Disney films, an experience that made a deep impression on him and which finds constant echoes in his own movies. 'Walt Disney was my parental conscience – and my step-parent was the TV set.' When asked as an adult about his cinematic influences, he stated:

> I don't think I've learned from any one film or filmmaker. When you've been exposed to film as much as I have, then certainly you're going to be influenced by films and directors you respond to. Every work is derivative of other stimuli, of course, but I haven't been able to sit down and say that *Close Encounters* is more like Capra or that *Jaws* is like Hitchcock or anything like that. Everyone is influenced, but in a very diffuse way.

When pressed further, however, he was prepared to admit that 'actually, I was probably more influenced by Walt Disney than by anybody else. I loved cartoons as a kid, and I remember that I was more frightened by the 'Night on Bald Mountain' sequence in *Fantasia* [1940] than by anything I ever saw in a movie before or since.' Indeed, many of his films contain Disney references: the mountain imagery of *Close Encounters* is reminiscent of *Fantasia*, *E.T.* has elements of *Bambi* (the forest scenes) and *Pinocchio* (E.T. hides amongst the toys to evade detection). This influence fuelled Spielberg's determination to see Hollywood return to making full-length animated feature films in the Disney style following the death of Uncle Walt and indeed he helped to restore their popularity by producing *An American Tail* (1986), and its 1990 sequel, and *Who Framed Roger Rabbit?* (1988), the latter with the Disney Empire's filmmaking arm, Touchstone Pictures. *Hook* was in many respects a non-animated sequel to Disney's *Peter Pan* (1953), a courageous project which perhaps inevitably drew unfavourable comparisons with the original cartoon classic. The interesting thing about Spielberg's love and admiration of Disney films is that therein lies a clue to his aspirations. For Spielberg, Disney's work stands like a monument to excellence and consistency to which he is constantly aspiring. Disney, in other words, built the mountain he is trying to climb.

Home, as the cliche has it, is where the heart is. And Spielberg's heart has long rested in his childhood. Returning there is like going home. His earliest memory – as impressive for its vividness as any of his films, especially as he was only six months old – is that of being wheeled in his pram down the aisle of a synagogue in Cincinatti. He typically describes the memory in cinematic terms. Out of the darkness, like a tracking shot, came a burst of red light. Bathed in it, in silhouette, were bearded men handing biscuits to him; Hasidic elders, wise old sages, bringing comfort and reassurance after the fear and wonder. Spielberg did not, however, have a particularly orthodox Jewish upbringing. Although his mother now runs a kosher delicatessen in West Los Angeles ('The Milky Way'), she was not then so strict on Steven's dietary habits. They shared, for example, a love of lobster and he tells with relish a story of how they were once almost caught cooking some by their rabbi on a house-call and Steven had to hide the clacking creatures under his bed until the visitor had gone, whereupon the delicacies were tossed into the cooking pot. This combined sense of terror and mischief surfaces in virtually all of his films. His childhood was 'the most fruitful period of my life', providing an Aladdin's Cave of memories, ideas and stories from which he constantly draws to make his films.

Spielberg's mother, Leah, was a considerable influence on his life. She was a former concert pianist who would help the boy develop his interests in filmmaking, rarely venturing into his bedroom except to collect his laundry (she hated his pet parakeets). 'Most kids are suspicious of adults, but my mother was just like another big kid to us. Such energy. And encouragement – she made everything fun.' To cater for Steven's growing obsession, on one occasion she cooked a cherries jubilee in a pressure cooker until it exploded so that her son could film the red, gooey mess all over the kitchen. 'The image I have of her,' he said many years later as though he was describing Julie Andrews in *The Sound of Music*, 'is of this tiny woman climbing to the top of a mountain, standing there with her arms out spinning around':

> My Mom was just like a little girl who never grew out of her pinafore. The rest of us just trailed after her: Dad and my three younger sisters and me. She left a large wake.

The feeling was apparently mutual. She recalled that she 'just hung on for dear life. He was always the centre of attention, ruling his three younger sisters. And me too, actually. Our living room was strewn with cables and floodlights – that's where Steven did his filming. We never said no. We never had a chance to say no. Steven didn't understand that word.' If he did, one suspects that he would have been unable to avoid the disturbing reality of his parents' estrangement by resorting to his imagination. 'All movies are wishful thinking,' he once said. 'In many of my films I find I have created the family warmth I wish I had experienced.'

It is, therefore, of considerable help in understanding Spielberg's films if we look at his childhood in some detail, a period of his life he has always been quite willing to talk about openly. Spielberg has described himself as a child as being 'the weird skinny kid with acne. I was a wimp.' He tried to improve his physique by doing chin-ups in the garage but, despite his hyper-activity and boundless energy, he could never channel it into sporting activities. Instead, he lived inside his imagination. Such behaviour was not likely to earn him many brownie points among his schoolmates. Hopeless at games, he was nicknamed 'the retard' by his more macho classmates, who made fun of him, especially when he was sickened by the thought of having to dissect a frog in biology class (literally, as he found himself vomiting outside with others – 'and the others were all girls'). Spielberg exorcised this memory in *E.T.* when he had Elliott free the frogs intended for dissection in his school biology class. He loved animals and shared his bedroom with parakeets that flew freely around him and his imaginary friend from outer space: 'I would show him my toys and he would show me his toys, and life wouldn't be so lonely.' Part of the reason for his loneliness was that, because his father's job required him to move around the country so much, just when the frightened little boy was becoming accepted by his schoolmates, it was time to move on again. His father, Arnold, was a workaholic electrical engineer, part of the team that designed the first computers.

Even as an adult making movies, he finds it difficult to cope with the parting of a team with whom he has worked closely over the prolonged period of time, perhaps even a year, that it takes to make a movie. 'At the end of that year everybody gets other jobs and they go off to Europe, they go off to New York, they go off to the South, they just scatter. Cast and crew members break up. It's a real sad moment for me.' This sense of sadness at parting was perhaps filmed to greatest effect in the final scene of *E.T.* when young Elliott has to say goodbye to his alien friend. As a child, Spielberg hated to leave the place he had just begun to feel comfortable in. 'At the moment of my greatest comfort and tranquillity, we'd move somewhere else . . . And the older I got, the harder it got.' Again, he tried to exorcise this and a whole host of other phobias during his *Amazing Stories* TV series. In an episode entitled 'Moving Day', an apparently normal suburban American teenage boy with an inventor father discovers that he is really part of an observation team from another planet when instructions arrive to move on to their next assignment – a planet that the boy has seen in his dreams. The difficulties of having to

Four teenagers look in awe to see a spaceship in Spielberg's *E.T. The Extra-Terrestrial*, 1982. Through the role of Elliot, Spielberg reveals many of his own childhood experiences and memories, including his ambiguous relationship with his teenage peers.

leave the teenage world he was just getting used to are compensated for by guarantees of the even better world that the new planet has to offer - with its promised rocket sleds rather than his denied motor bikes – and the discovery that his Earth girlfriend will be joining him on the journey to his parents' next assignment: 'Guess what my parents told me tonight?' she says in the final line as he realizes that she is also an alien in the same boat.

Wherever Spielberg's bedroom was, it served as his psychological cave. There, he could escape from his loneliness, his boredom, his bullying schoolmates, from family rows – from reality. When, for example, his parents gave him those pet birds:

I took the parakeets out of their little jail and trained them to live on the curtain rod. At one time there were eight parakeets living on that rod, dripping like candles in old Italian restaurants. After a while, it changes the whole fabric of the curtains . . . I'd find a name I like – say Schmuck – and just give the birds other sequel names: Schmuck II, Schmuck III. No imagination [!]

Every now and again, having hatched up one of his 'unimaginative' little plots he would emerge from his room to play practical jokes on his three mischievous younger sisters as a way of cajoling them into appearing in his home movies, again placing this on record in *Poltergeist* which was 'all about the terrible things I did to my younger sisters'. That film was also all about the terrible things that he let his imagination do to himself. He was, for example, most frightened by one of their clown dolls, but also by cracks in the wall in which he thought people lived, or by ghosts that would emerge from the closet, by creepy-crawlies under the bed, by wind monsters or trees with tentacles outside the bedroom window – and a whole host of typical childhood phobias that have fuelled scenes in this and his other movies. As he has admitted: 'You saw my house when you saw *Close Encounters*, *Poltergeist* and *E.T.* . . . . The house in *E.T.* is very much like the house I was raised in. That's my bedroom! And the little girl, Gertie, is an amalgamation of my three, terrifying sisters.' Finding suburbia too boring for his liking, he retreated into his fantasies, admitting that this was the furnace that fired his films:

> It's a result of where I grew up, in suburbia, in Phoenix, Arizona. It was a place where excitement was nowhere to be found and you had to create it yourself if you wanted to enjoy your teenage years. I started making movies when I was 12. It came out of boredom, and that's why I joined the boy scouts when I learned how to make films. There was a photography merit badge I wanted to achieve and I learned how to make films. I made a little movie on my dad's 8mm camera, even though the rules said you had to tell a story with still photographs. Once I could make films, I found I could 'create' a great day or a great week just by creating a story: I could synthesize my life. It's just the same reason writers get started, so that they can improve the world or fix it. I found I could do anything or live anywhere via my imagination, through film.

One particular formative event took place when he was six. He recalled that his father rushed home in the middle of the night, bundled the family into the war surplus jeep and drove them to a nearby field where hundreds of neighbours were staring at a meteor storm in the night sky. His father 'gave me a technical explanation of what was happening . . . But I didn't want to hear that. I wanted to think of them as falling stars.' Thus were sown the seeds for a scene in *Close Encounters* that recreates this experience almost exactly as Steven remembered it.

But first he had to start small. More appalled than tolerant at his father's clumsy attempts at home movies and feeling he could do better, the 12 year old appointed himself the family's official cinematographer. Before long he began to experiment, filming toy train crashes, the night sky, the pet dog that frightened him – setting up shots, trying different techniques, dreaming up storylines. An example of his instinctive feel for the medium at such a young age was when he realized that he could build up the tension for his toy train crash by filming his train moving from left to right from one side and from right to left on the other. *Escape to Nowhere*, a 40-minute fully scripted war film made in 1961, was his first effort at a substantial project and about 15 other small films followed over the next few years (now mostly lost), all financed by whitewashing citrus trees in his spare time. Primitive dubbing and editing were also tried. Once he had commandeered his father's 8mm Kodak movie camera, he discovered that he could not only reinterpret his father's scientific explanations by making science fiction films, including one two-and-a-half-hour epic called *Firelight* about a team of scientists investigating mysterious lights in the night sky, made when he was 16 and starring the entire family, but he could also escape from the unhappiness caused by the world around him. 'I used film, I think, to escape into a world of fantasy. Away from my parents . . . They weren't getting along and there was a lot of noise in the house at night. It was an escape for me. A great escape'. By then, he had discovered that he could also defuse bullying at school through his little films, even casting one of his more persistent adversaries in a film called *Battle Squad*, with the result that he became his friend and protector.

> He was my nemesis; I dreamed about him. Then I figured, if you can't beat him, try to get him to join you. So I said to him, 'I'm making this movie about fighting the Nazis and I want you to play this war hero.' At first he laughed in my face, but later he said yes. He was this big 14 year old who looked like John Wayne. I made him the squad leader in the film, with helmet, fatigues and backpack. After that he became my best friend.

Firelight was shown in a local Phoenix cinema for one night only (his father had rented it) and the $500 epic made a profit of $100: his first real box office success.

Further peer approval had already been achieved through his film-making talents, such as his admission into the secret school honor society 'The Order of the Arrow'. But none of these successes eradicated prior unhappy memories. In one of his *Amazing Stories* ('The Main Attraction', directed by Mathew Robbins) a vain, spoiled high school jock's house is hit in a meteor storm, whereupon he is literally magnetized. But so is an unglamorous 'nerdish' girl who has a crush on him and whom he spends all his time trying to avoid. Spielberg's adult revenge on all his teenage bullies was to have them literally pulled together as opposite poles attract.

As in this mid-eighties television series, Spielberg the boy would spend hours in his introspective world devising his stories and filming his home movies, planning them out from storyboard to final edit. *E.T.* began life as this slightly isolated boy's 'invisible friend'. As *Time Magazine's* tribute to him put it in 1982, 'film-making has been a profitable form of psychotherapy' for Spielberg. Or, as the same magazine put it in 1985, 'each picture has allowed him to remake his own childhood, then to generalize it so it touches millions of once-again kids'.

Not surprisingly, Spielberg hated school – developing in the process an almost cynical realization that through filmmaking he could manipulate people quite easily. With film, he could do this with positive rather than negative results. School work interfered with his growing obsession, which was certainly his way of disarming his childhood fears, exorcising them and thereby transferring them onto others. It was also his way of asserting his personality. In a female-dominated household ('Even the dog was female') 'I had to do something to make my presence felt. I used to do anything in my imagination to terrify them.' He would also rent films and turn the living room into a mini-cinema, with Mom and his sisters making popcorn; the first time he did this as a means of raising money to make his own films he made $36 but then asked his mother to drive him to the local handicapped school so that he could donate his profits. The much teased Spielberg did in fact recognize the importance of looking after those less fortunate than himself; he even deliberately fell in a school race to let a handicapped boy cross the line ahead of him, as all the other boys cheered and laughed at his defeat. 'I'd never felt better and I'd never felt worse in my entire life,' he recalled.

Once he joined the Boy Scouts to secure the photography merit badge the quest quite literally consumed and channelled his adolescent passions:

> I'm not saying that being sheltered is a good thing, that it's good for kids who live in the outskirts not really to get a sense of what it's like to be a person in a real world of movement and energy and, in many ways, of hostility. But if I hadn't been a Scout I'd probably have ended up as an axe murderer or a butcher in a Jewish deli.

As an Eagle Scout, he quickly began to gain in confidence and improve his film technique while, at Phoenix's Arcadia High School, he joined the theatre arts programme, 'my leper colony', where he 'discovered that there were options beside being a jock or a wimp'. This was by no means his only childhood dilemma. Another, reflected in many of his films, was whether to concentrate on the arts or the sciences – a conflict which he partly derived from his parents. In 1958, his father brought home a tiny transistor, declaring: 'this is the future'. The 11-year-old Spielberg examined it carefully – and promptly swallowed it. Not for the first time did Spielberg recall a very vivid childhood memory as though it was a scene from an old movie. 'Dad laughed', Spielberg recalled,

> then he didn't laugh; it got very tense. It was like the confrontation scene between Raymond Massey and James Dean in *East of Eden*. One of those moments when two diametrically opposed positions in the universe collide. It was as if I was saying: 'That's your future, but it doesn't have to be mine'.

Although his father tried to push Steven into academic directions he had already decided against, tolerating his son's obsessive amateur filmmaking only so long as his school reports were up to scratch, Arnold's growing absenteeism from the family home was partly a reflection of his work demands and partly of his growing estrangement from his wife.

> My father had a map he tried to get me to follow. He wanted me to be an electrical engineer or a doctor so he was very strict with me regarding all the high school courses that would lead me in those directions, such as maths or chemistry, which I was intuitively horrible at. Of course I took the opposite trail and followed in my mother's footsteps.

This was perhaps inevitable with his father working away so often and, as a result, Spielberg grew up surrounded by females. Even in adult life, he surrounds himself with female company. 'I work better with women', he once said. 'I claim no profound understanding of women, but I have an agreeable faith in them.' He has (inevitably!) been criticized for being patronizing towards women in his films, but his female screen characters are all slightly ambivalent and reveal a great deal about his attitude towards his sisters or his mother. In Spielberg's film families the mother figure is invariably strong and resourceful (as in *Gremlins*, demonstrated by the way in which she handles herself superbly in the kitchen), emotional and slightly whimsical, yet protective (as in *E.T.* and *Poltergeist*) or alienated from the husband (as in *Close Encounters*). In *Jaws*, Spielberg abandoned the book's plotline of an affair between Brody's wife and Hooper for the film. Equally, the screen fathers are a little more obsessive (as in *Close Encounters*), conservative (as in *Poltergeist*), elusive or enigmatic (as in *1941* and *Last Crusade*), or simply absent (as in *E.T.*, or *Empire of the Sun* and *The Color Purple* – in the last two of which both parents were mostly absent). In his first feature, *The Sugarland Express*, both parents were criminals.

The degree to which these various portrayals are directly relevant to Spielberg's own perceptions is varied. Arnold Spielberg has said: 'I'd help Steven construct sets for his 8mm movies, with toy trucks and papier mâché mountains' – an event echoed in *Close Encounters* when the father becomes obsessive about building a papier mâché mountain. The personality clashes between his parents grew wider through Spielberg's adolescence. He the scientist and she the artist gave Spielberg a 'circuit overload':

> My tweeters would burn out and my only insulation would be my bedroom door, which remained closed for most of my life. I had to put towels under the jamb so I couldn't hear the classical music and the computer logic.

Most children in such circumstances do either of two things: they either face the realities or they blot them out, often developing into disturbed adults as a result. That young Steven was able to avoid this was due in no small part to his ability to escape into fantasy via film.

When he was 16, the family moved from Phoenix to Saratoga, a suburb of San José in Northern California, now part of 'Silicon Valley'. There, Spielberg's parents separated and then divorced in 1965. Perhaps reflecting his predisposition to romanticize his childhood, undoubtedly attempting to make as an adult the best out of traumatic memories, he said:

> They [his parents] hung in there to protect us until we were old enough. But I don't think that they were aware of how acutely aware we were of their unhappiness – not violence, just a pervading unhappiness you could cut with a fork or a spoon at dinner every night. For years I thought the word 'divorce' was the ugliest in the English language. Sound travelled from bedroom to bedroom, and the word came seeping through the heating ducts. My sisters and I would stay up at night, listening to our parents argue, hiding from that word. And when it travelled into our room, absolute abject panic set in. My sisters would burst into tears, and we would all hold one another. And when the separation finally came, we were no better off for having waiting six years for it to occur.

In the first of the *Back to the Future* films, the bullied kid (played by Michael J. Fox) travels back into the past in an effort to patch up his parents' failing courtship – yet one more example of how Spielberg attempts to recreate his own life through film. But in retrospect, he did manage to overcome his sense of regret at his parents divorce: 'I'm really happy for my childhood. I had a full 15 years with my parents. Today, by 12, kids are essentially independent. They don't sense the kind of camaraderies we had.'

The move to California was to prove fateful, especially when in 1965 he visited Universal Studios as part of a tourist party. Legends abound (mostly, it has to be said, originating from Spielberg himself) concerning what really followed but the least inconsistent of his versions runs as follows. The 17-year old Spielberg broke away from the main tourist party to see the sound stages where he bumped into the head of Universal's editorial department, Chuck Silvers. 'Instead of calling the guards to throw me off the lot, he talked to me for about an hour . . . . He said he'd like to see some of my little films, and so he gave me a pass to get on the lot the next day.' When he duly turned up, Silvers said he was impressed but could do no more for him except wish him luck. Undeterred, Spielberg the following day put on a suit, borrowed his father's briefcase and walked straight through the front gate as though he did this all the time. The guard ('Scotty') apparently mistook him for the son of Lew Wassermann, the head of MCA–Universal.

> So every day that summer, I went in my suit and hung out with directors and writers and editors and dubbers. I found an office that wasn't being used and became a squatter. I went to a camera store, bought some plastic name titles and put my name in the building directory. Steven Spielberg, Room 22C.

Such nerve failed, however, to bring its immediate rewards; 'actually, it was a cul-de-sac experience for me because, once in, I discovered that nobody really wanted anything I had to offer, that it was still a middle-aged man's profession.' He simply couldn't get anyone else to look at his films.

The following autumn, he went to California State University at Long Beach. He naturally wanted to study film, but his high school grades were not sufficiently good to get him into a major film school such as USC or UCLA. He had, therefore, to content himself with studying English, chosen perhaps because he was only too aware of his literary shortcomings. 'I did begin by reading comics; I did see too many movies; I did, still do, watch too much television. I feel the lack of having been raised on good literature and the written word.' Inevitably, however, he found himself sitting in cinemas rather than in libraries and he began making films on 16mm, financed by part-time jobs, before being drawn back to the Universal Studios lot – in fact for three days a week where he would study filmmakers at work, including Alfred Hitchcock. He was apparently thrown off the set of *Torn Curtain* (1965) by an assistant director.

A workaholic with regard to his extracurricular activities, his university studies inevitably suffered while he hustled and bustled to get his films seen by Universal's executives.

> They were embarrassed when I asked them to remove their pictures from the wall so that I could project my little silent movies. They said, 'If you

make your films in 16mm or, even better, 35mm, then they'll get seen. So I immediately went to work in the college commissary to earn the money to buy 16mm film and rent a camera. I had to get those films seen.

The result was *Amblin'*, a 22-minute film with no dialogue about a boy and a girl hitch-hiking from the desert to the Pacific, made at a cost of $10,000 in ten days and financed by a wealthy college friend (Dennis Hoffman) who wanted to become a movie producer. It was a very slick production, being photographed by Allen Daviau (who was to be Spielberg's cameraman on *E.T.*) – although in later life he refers to it as 'an attack of crass commercialism' and dismisses it as 'a Pepsi commercial'. He feels it demonstrates how apathetic he was in the 1960s while others of his age were fighting in Vietnam or protesting at Kent State University: '*Amblin'* is the slick by-product of a kid immersed up to his nose in film', he admitted. Even so, it worked in so far as it got him noticed.

> I had made a lot of little films in 16mm that were getting me nowhere. They were very esoteric. I wanted to shoot something that could prove to people who finance movies that I could certainly look like a professional moviemaker. *Amblin'* was a conscious effort to break into the business and become successful by proving to people I could move a camera and compose nicely and deal with lighting and performances.

The day after it was shown by Chuck Silvers at Universal, he was summoned by a highly impressed Sidney Jay Sheinberg, then head of Universal's TV Production, who gave him that historic seven-year contract which he came to resent so much. 'Sir, I liked your work,' said the formal Sheinberg to the now 21 year-old Spielberg. 'How would you like to go to work professionally?' 'I quit college so fast,' said Spielberg, 'I didn't even clean out my locker.' Although he feared his father would never forgive him for not graduating, he was in fact entering the University of Television, the experience of which was to serve him well in his chosen career (as it had such film directors before him as Arthur Penn and Robert Altman). That he might just have done the right thing became evident when *Amblin'* won the Atlanta Film Festival award and another award at Venice in 1969, and was paired with *Love Story* for national distribution in 1970.

It was not long before Spielberg the college drop-out was actually being studied by college film students. Indeed, several years later, following the release of *The Sugarland Express*, he was giving a seminar to some students visiting Universal. One of them recalled: 'We walked into his office and this kid walked in. After the class I hung back and said to him 'I have this student film. Would you like to see it?' Remembering his own frustration at trying to get his early films seen by people on the inside of the business, Spielberg watched the opportunist's film, *Field of Honor*, and loved it. 'My God, it was spectacular for a film student in his early twenties to have made such a picture for no money . . . This man is worth watching.' The young director was Robert Zemeckis whom Spielberg hired to direct his first two incursions into production, *I Wanna Hold Your Hand* (1978), about six teenagers who travel to New York to see the Beatles appear on 'The Ed Sullivan Show', and *Used Cars* (1980) as well as the more lucrative *Back to the Future* films. The third film that Spielberg was to produce, *Continental Divide* (1981, directed by Michael Apted) introduced him to the scriptwriting skills of Lawrence Kasdan, whom Spielberg hired to write *Raiders of the Lost Ark* and who was himself to emerge as a director of considerable merit with *Body Heat* (1982), *The Big Chill* (1983) and *Silverado* (1985).

This talent-spotting is one way Spielberg repays the industry that he cares so much about and that has made him a multi-millionaire. He was himself helped enormously during his early period in the late 1960s and early 1970s (and indeed subsequently) by a group of talented young filmmakers, which included George Lucas (*Star Wars*) and Francis Ford Coppola (*The Godfather*), plus the writers John Milius (co-writer of *Magnum Force* and *Apocalypse Now!*), Paul Schrader (*Taxi Driver, Blue Collar, American Gigolo, Raging Bull, Cat People*), Hal Barwood and Mathew Robbins (Spielberg's credited writers on *The Sugarland Express* and uncredited collaborators on all his early films). Coppola, however, was the model, 'my shining star' because

> here was a student from UCLA who was writing professionally, who was making a living from his writing, and just starting out as a director with Roger Corman . . . So in a way, Francis was the first inspiration to a lot of young filmmakers, because he broke through before many others.

He also later became friends with Martin Scorsese (*Alice Doesn't Live Here Anymore, Taxi Driver, Mean Streets*, etc) and Brian De Palma (*Carrie, The Untouchables*). Although grouped together as 'the Movie Brats' they were in fact too diverse a group to be simply lumped together in this way. But as friends, they would exchange scripts, ideas and rough cuts 'like kids exchanging baseball cards' as Spielberg put it. They learned from each other, bounced off one another, criticized one another. Spielberg and De Palma were among the small select group to whom Lucas decided to first unveil the rough cut – minus special effects – of *Star Wars* in 1977. Spielberg helped Scorsese edit the final ten minutes of *Taxi Driver* in 1976. Filmmaker friends suggested he blow up the shark at the end of *Jaws*. 'We've all helped each other with our movies,' he said, and constructive criticism helped make their movies even better. As young men in an ageing profession, they found advice from each other when none was forthcoming from elsewhere.

Spielberg, who had earlier been thrown out of an editing room by Mervyn Le Roy, was even escorted off the set when he again tried to watch Hitchcock working, this time making *Family Plot* (1976), even though he had just finished *Jaws*. 'I just desperately wanted to watch him working and now I guess I never will,' he said after the death of one of his mentors. As his own contemporary circle all became more experienced, they became less inclined to run these rough-cut preview sessions. They needed less help than they did when they were younger and, besides, as they all got older, they tended to become more critical of each other's work – and more sensitive.

A glance at the filmography will reveal just how much Spielberg utilizes the same crew members on many of his films. This is to some extent playing safe with the people he knows he can work with, such as John Williams, Michael Kahn and Douglas Slocombe. In his early television days, when he was patronized by older, hardened and often less talented professionals as well as being forced to work on projects he didn't like in ways he didn't approve of, he resolved that would become, in a sense, more autocratic as a director.

> I've had a few bummer experiences where people touted as the best turned out to be empty-headed and riding on empty reputations. I'm leery when a person is highly touted. I must work with him to know what he can really do. Actually, I've had the best luck with people off the street – relatively new people working in film.

He doesn't, therefore, suffer fools lightly; provided he can work with energetic and imaginative people, he is open to all kinds of suggestions on his film projects. Although single-minded about the film's concept, he recognizes that filmmaking is not a one-man band:

> Whatever I do, I do through other people. But I guess I'm not the most fun to work with unless the people I hire can sit on their egos. When I plan a sequence, I see the locations and plan where the camera goes, so essentially it's already shot and edited. In the planning stage, I'm a story-teller, a cinematographer and an editor. *Then* I have to work with people and get it all across to them.

The only areas he will not be moved on are camera positions and editing, 'because camera positions and editing is what it's all about. Beyond that, I'm open to collaboration.'

.

There have, however, been several unfortunate experiences in collaboration. There has been talk of Spielberg rowing with Verna Fields, the Oscar-winning editor of *Jaws*, with Paul Schrader who worked on the early script of *Close Encounters*, and with his early producers such as Zanuck and Brown and Mike and Julia Phillips. Personality clashes amongst dedicated, creative people are perhaps inevitable, especially when the pressures of working in a multi-million dollar business are added to the collaborative artistic business of filmmaking. Latterly in his career, Spielberg has managed to keep such clashes to a minimum by working with people he knows he can trust and who are on the same wavelength. But even as a producer, he still found it difficult to relinquish control over his visions. This became particularly apparent during the making of *Poltergeist* in 1982.

Because he was so engrossed with *E.T.* at the time, Spielberg decided to employ Tobe Hooper of *Texas Chainsaw Massacre* fame (1974) to direct his 'revenge on television'. As a horror movie in which a suburban Californian family home is infiltrated by malevolent spirits via the television set, the film is in fact typically Spielberg – with its suburban setting, its Disney and other old film references on television (including one to the 1944 Spencer Tracy film *A Guy Named Joe*, which he was to 'rework' as *Always*), its menacing tree, its resourceful mother and its invisible windlike presence, which captures the little sister. This does beg the question as to how much influence the producer had over the director in the making of the film. A controversy blew up when Spielberg's name as producer appeared in larger print on the trailer than Hooper's.

What had happened was that Spielberg had written the original story and then handed his 50-page treatment to writers Michael Grais and Mark Victor, planning as always to go off to Hawaii and build a huge sandcastle to commemorate the completion of another film. 'But when I found they had written a movie that didn't work for me, I sat down at home and wrote a whole new movie in five days.' This work blitz served as a catharsis for Spielberg to exorcise many of his childhood fears and fantasies and 'I suddenly became more parent to the project than I'd ever anticipated.' He continued:

> I just fell in love with the project. I couldn't help myself. And when the film started shooting I was on the set every day . . . I began to watch where the camera was going, make sure it was going in the right position. I story-boarded the movie and after I had finished selecting the story-boards, I would pass them on to Tobe and he had every right to change them but he never did. Even George Lucas doesn't hang around the set when he hires

other directors. But this was my baby and I loved the experience of working on the film.

Once Hooper had made the final cut, Spielberg edited the picture 'and it turned out my way'. Then the controversy blew up, with Spielberg's enemies accusing him of egotistical tyrannical tendencies, whereupon he had to take out advertisements in the trade journals thanking Hooper for his contribution. 'My taking over,' he said, 'had less to do with Tobe's competence and more with the fact that I'm bullish about my ideas.' But he learned an important lesson from *Poltergeist*, namely 'that I will never write something that I don't direct. I will never again give away something I write.' This was one more episode that forced Spielberg to adopt a thicker skin in order to protect himself from the harsh realities of the outside world.

He also had to face the knives that were out for him during the filming of the 'Kick the Can' segment of *The Twilight Zone – The Movie*, a four-episode film homily to one of his favourite television shows, which he co-produced in 1983. Spielberg had already worked for Serling's 'Night Gallery' series in his early television days. Of his predecessor, Spielberg has gone on record as saying that 'I think *The Twilight Zone* was probably the most phenomenal half-hour, and then hour, *ever* to air as a science fiction/fantasy anthology':

> Many endings were almost lessons to the world, chafing across the knuckles. Some shows were actually rather cynical, and I really enjoyed that – it was a sign of the times, and it was what kids talked about Monday morning when they went back to school.

Following the success of *Raiders* and of *E.T.*, he was able to persuade Warner Brothers to let him and some of his grown up director pals (John Landis of *Blues Brothers* fame – in which Spielberg appeared briefly – Joe Dante, who had made *The Howling* and who was to make the two *Gremlins* films for Spielberg, and George Miller, maker of the *Mad Max* films) pay their own filmic tribute to the old Rod Serling series.

Spielberg's directoral contribution in the 1983 film is not particularly effective but, through its plot concerning an elderly romantic who contrives a method of allowing old people to return to their childhood, with all its associated pains as well as its pleasures, he is able to project his view that life is about being your age while keeping the mind young and fresh. The philosophy about being as young as you feel was taken further in one episode of *Amazing Stories* directed by Robert Markowitz entitled 'Magic Saturday' in which a young boy allows his physically ailing but mentally youthful grandfather to swop bodies so that he can recapture the baseball glories of his youth. While grandfather is enjoying his new lease of life in the boy's body (winning friends and admirers for the wimpish kid in the process) the boy finds he has occupied a dying shell and the tension is caused by the struggle to get the two together again so that they can return to their rightful places. The *Amazing Stories* series was originally scheduled to be 44 episodes but, following mixed reviews and relatively low ratings, the notoriously fickle television executives cancelled the series after 24 episodes.

This was by no means his first set-back, and it will probably not be his last. During the filming of the segment of *The Twilight Zone* directed by John Landis, two children and the actor Vic Morrow were killed in a helicopter accident in July 1982. Coming so soon after the release of *E.T.*, the tragedy – especially the deaths of two young Vietnamese children, aged six and seven, who were working illegally in the early hours of the morning – tarnished the image of the film's co-producer, even though

Scatman Crothers (*centre*) offers the proverbial Fountain of Youth to the despondent residents of a rest-house, telling them how a child's game can make them young again in *The Twilight Zone – The Movie*, 1983. Segment directed by Spielberg.

Spielberg himself was nowhere near the set, 40 miles north of Los Angeles, when the Bell C-205 crashed. A series of law suits and official investigations followed, and although Spielberg was exonerated and exempted from the eventual fines for violation of the child labour laws, hostility was something that he was having to become increasingly used to. His fame and success prompted all sorts of weird and not so wonderful claims that he had stolen someone's idea for each and (nearly) every one of his films. Moreover, seemingly at the peak of his career in 1982 as his masterpiece crashed through every box-office record world-wide, claims emerged that he had stolen the idea for *E.T.* from a little known musical called *Lokey from Maldemar*. This, combined with the *Poltergeist* controversy (followed by the murder of one of its stars, Dominique Dunne) and *The Twilight Zone* accident and subsequent investigations, all served as a watershed for Spielberg personally. Reality was forcing him to grow up rather faster than he would have wished; the real world had finally invaded his fantasy world with a vengeance.

In the late 1980s, following almost a decade as a movie producer, with all its constant headaches and problems, Spielberg decided to reduce his activities in this respect and hand them over to Kathleen Kennedy and Frank Marshall. Production had become too much like going to school for him in that he was being forced to work on subjects that he was not interested in. Moreover, he hated interfering in the work of the directors he had hired, which was often necessary for him as a businessman. He wanted to go back to directing and, indeed, 1989 was the first time two films directed by Spielberg came out in a single year.

An even-tempered workaholic who oftens works 20 hours a day and who does not smoke, drink, take drugs or use the casting couch, Steven Spielberg is a man-child whose adulthood has never quite proved as satisfying as his childhood. Given that he has so often commented on how unhappy he was as a child, this might suggest a rather sad character. He has gone on record as saying that 'the only time I feel totally happy is when I'm watching films or making them', although in later life he has drawn enormous pleasure from his children from different relationships. He is a video games fanatic – he plays them for at least one hour every day in his offices or at home – which one suspects is a major way of releasing his tension (although recent research has demonstrated that video games can affect the young mind in highly creative and educational ways). At Amblin Entertainment, a Mexican-style office complex built for him in 1984 to his own design in the grounds of Universal Studios by MCA in gratitude for the success of *E.T.*, he is regarded as a pleasant boss, courteous, very relaxed, always consulting, always buzzing. He is undoubtedly a dreamer and he has fantasized about being the first civilian

Spielberg in characteristic baseball cap during the filming of *The Color Purple*, 1985. During the 1980s, he produced more films than he directed through his company Amblin Entertainment, which brought with it a sense of economic reality. But he is only really happy behind the camera. As his friend Martin Scorsese has said: 'Directing is what Steven has to do'.

NASA takes into space on the shuttle. He dresses casually – usually jeans, sweatshirt, characteristic baseball cap and training shoes – reflecting his generally unflamboyant personality.

Although he has been unspoiled by success, the nature of his business now requires him to be tough and often very single-minded. 'You have to ride people hard,' he says. 'You have to say things more than once. About the third time you get what you want.' This has led to several acrimonious clashes with people he has worked with, denting his halo. Even now, he survives on his fears – anticipating being trapped in a lift or his Malibu beach house sliding into the sea (it in fact burned down in 1988) or the audience reaction to his next movie. He still bites his nails – he has done since he was four – 'it's my only vice'. He can suffer from bouts of depression but, as he says:

> I do my best work when I'm in the pits emotionally. Sometimes I'm in the pits for six months straight, but it's okay because my creative juices don't flow as well when I'm happy.

He has admitted that he doesn't 'like being an adult' and he has certainly found the transition difficult on a personal level, especially after the break-up of his first marriage to the actress Amy Irving whom he married after the birth of his first son, Max, in 1985. While bringing from him an enormous amount of paternal love and prompting his more 'adult' phase, a temporary casualty of this process was his long-standing project to make a film about *Peter Pan* which he said in 1987:

> We were all ready to go; John Williams had already written nine songs. Then Max, my son, was born and the last thing I wanted was to raise nine kids in London, hanging on wires against a blue-screen special effect device, instead of being with my own son, raising *him*. And I think I lost interest in that theme of the boy who refuses to grow up. I was 40 this year and I guess something changed. There's nothing I love more than making movies, but now there's another kind of love. If I had to give it up for my son, I really believe I would.

One might have thought that his own teenage experience, combined with his hatred of relocation, would have motivated him to resist divorce as strongly as possible but 'irreconcilable differences' with Max's mother and the separations caused by independent movie careers resulted in an 'amicable' though highly publicized £59 million divorce settlement in April 1989. He is currently married to Kate Capshaw, the lead female star of *Temple of Doom* and with whom he had his second son in 1990.

The message that emerges from his films is that good will triumph in the end provided people are determined enough to overcome their fears. He concedes that people have genuine cause to be afraid but that it is when they let it get the better of them that they are in the most danger of being overwhelmed. For a man who is almost unparalleled in his ability to evoke emotion in his audiences and who gets his characters to follow their instincts, his is a rationalist philosophy: the heart is essential to the mind and body, but it is in the head where ultimately decisions have to be made – whether it be Elliot's decision to stay in *E.T.* or Roy's decision to go in *Close Encounters*. Mister's decision to allow Nettie's return to Celie in *The Color Purple* is motivated in the end by rational self-

Spielberg with his first wife, Amy Irving, at the Golden Globe Awards in Los Angeles. Despite their much publicized divorce in 1989, Spielberg tries to protect his private life from the glare of publicity, including his second marriage to Kate Capshaw. This contrasts with his willingness to talk about his own ideas and experiences at the drop of a hat.

interest. Brody, the man who overcomes his fears, and Hooper, the man who overcomes his naivety, survive in *Jaws*, whereas Quint, who cannot overcome his hatred, does not. Jim, in *Empire of the Sun*, survives because he adjusts his loyalties to his circumstances. The 'Indiana Jones' trilogy is not, however, a series of films in which Spielberg's philosophy of life can easily by discerned, although it is a goldmine for Spielberg's philosophy of action-adventure filmmaking. Indiana Jones survives simply because he is Indiana Jones. *Always* reveals his intention to concentrate more on letting the characters tell the story, in the vein of *The Color Purple* and *Empire of the Sun*, rather than letting their personalities emerge through the action. *Hook* is a combination of both.

With a dozen films to his directorial credit so far, and with nearly twice that many productions, not to mention his historical contributions to American television, where next for Spielberg?

Whatever Spielberg decides to do, now that he has finally completed his film of Peter Pan, if he is to be dragged out of his childhood, it will have to be kicking and screaming. But he will still have to try and operate within an industry dictated more and more by commercial pressures.

> And that's a blessing in disguise because it will bring us back to the story and the characters. It will compel us to return to the source of all great story-telling – the human soul and how it suffers and celebrates. Let's go back to finding out who we are – not necessarily what we are capable of constructing.

2

Spielberg and
the American Present

> I never want to release my movies. I want to keep working on them
> forever. They go into the theatres – and they suddenly cease to exist for
> me. Like something that died.

This statement reveals how deeply personal a filmmaker Spielberg is.
Once his films leave the studio and go on general release, they are for him
essentially like children who have grown up under his highly protective
care and have suddenly left home. It is that sorrow of parting again.
When his artistic creations enter the big wide world they also become
subject to all sorts of public pressures and interpretations over which he
has no control. Because he is every bit a part of the audience, his
nervousness stems from the fact that Spielberg is such a perfectionist that
he himself can never really be satisfied with one of his own creations. He
does what he can by steering the project through from idea to storyboard
to script to filming and to editing, but he remains insecure about the
public reaction because he is insecure about whether he himself has been
able to meet his own very high aspirations.

Spielberg's first four cinema releases, *Duel*, *The Sugarland Express*,
Jaws and *Close Encounters of the Third Kind* are distinctive in that they
are firmly set in the present day, that is near enough at the time they
were made. This is admittedly also true of *E.T. – The Extra Terrestrial*,
but that film, not only as cinema's most successful movie ever but also as
Spielberg's most deeply personal film, deserves a special chapter of its
own. *E.T.* was also made at a time when, following the huge success of
Jaws and *Close Encounters*, Spielberg was freer to make the films he
wanted to make and not be subject to the whims of producers. Even so,
in his first four projects, Spielberg was able to inject much of his

personality into those apprenticeship films and to experiment with techniques that have since become part of his filmmaking style.

As a young man learning and perfecting his craft, his concerns were initially more with the quality of his product than with anything else. His had been a life in films and filmmaking, protected from the outside world in his darkened cinemas and editing rooms. Even so, there are elements of a general outlook on life, an ideology if you like, that were to resurface in later films in a more developed form. Once films are released, they are, in a sense, public property, but any film analysis runs the risk of seeing things that are not there, of inventing interpretations that were not intended by the director. Though, despite his meticulous advance planning, Spielberg is such an instinctive filmmaker on the set that he himself might be unaware of the subconscious elements that permeate his films while he is making them. But he is also a careful filmmaker and this gives him plenty of time to work out precisely what he is doing. And although his films do provide a unified view of the universe, with that unity being identifiable by vast numbers of people who share the same vision, his films none the less provide images of contemporary concern and preoccupation that can be interpreted on a variety of different levels.

DUEL (1971)

Duel was originally made for television in America (being first screened on 13 November 1971) and was followed by two further TV movies, *Savage* and *Something Evil*. It was released in Europe, Australia and Japan as a feature film in 1973 and thus deserves to be grouped separately from his other early television work. Shot in 16 days for a mere $375,000, the programme had fewer than fifty lines of dialogue, and that much only because his producers would not accommodate Spielberg's initial desire to make a feature-length silent movie. For cinema release, it was extended by 15 minutes with three additional scenes and voice-over commentary by the star, Dennis Weaver. The first, in a series of road shots taken through the windscreen, showed Weaver starting out on his journey – the television version just begins on the open road. The second extra scene, written by producer Eckstein, showed Mann (Weaver) phoning home to apologise to his wife. Spielberg wanted this left out of the cinema print but was forced to keep it on the insistence of the distributors, CIC. 'I guess I was so enthusiastic about getting this film seen theatrically in the 1.85:1 ratio that I went ahead and shot the sequence . . .I don't think Weaver's character needed that kind of lead-pipe overkill.' The third scene was the memorable one in which

Mann's car, which has stopped for an endlessly passing train, is suddenly jolted forward as the truck tries to push him into the train's path. 'I loved the idea that the train and the truck were allied,' said Spielberg. It recouped $7 million at the box office and established for Spielberg a reputation that was to propel him headlong into feature filmmaking.

Only a year before the film was made, however, Spielberg was desperately unhappy fulfilling his Universal television contract. Having penetrated the entertainment industry, he found he was being squeezed out by the more experienced professionals. Very little work came his way following the disastrous reviews of his debut programme for 'Night Gallery'. He tried writing his own screenplays but found that he could not raise the money to make any of his own projects. After all, no one had heard of him – yet. He was forced, therefore, to make other people's films, with other people's choice of crews and casts and to a large extent felt he was merely churning out the kind of routine television that he had disliked so much when he was growing up in Phoenix. But then, risking the jibes of her colleagues, Spielberg's secretary Nona Tyson passed him a copy of *Playboy* magazine and urged him to turn to a short story by Richard Matheson, a veteran science fiction writer and contributor to *The Twilight Zone* television series. Spielberg knew immediately that he heen handed his first big break.

Duel tells the story of a suburban travelling salesman on his way to a meeting who is mysteriously menaced by an anonymous truck driver whose face we never see and whose motives are never explained. In 1986, Spielberg said that 'in all the years I've been making movies, I have not found anything as potentially frought with suspense and tension as *Duel*.' Matheson claimed to have based the story on a real life experience of his, and it appealed to Spielberg because he was reminded of his own teenage experiences while first driving his uncle's cumbersome 1957 Plymouth convertible on the Californian freeways. David Mann (played by Dennis Weaver), said Spielberg, 'is typical of that lower middle-class American who's insulated by suburban modernization. A man like that never expects to be challenged by anything more than his television set breaking down and having to call the repair man.' By placing this ordinary character in an extraordinary situation, Spielberg investigates his personal resources through confusion, terror, anger, paranoia and, finally, retribution. It locates ordinariness, places it precisely on the spot and, through crisis, teases resourcefulness from mediocrity.

Spielberg planned the film on a story-board that was 40 yards long and five feet high; 'it was really neat . . . it was a mural of the movie'. This helped him to visualize and plan out the film in advance – and to show his startled television producers, who had never seen anything quite like this

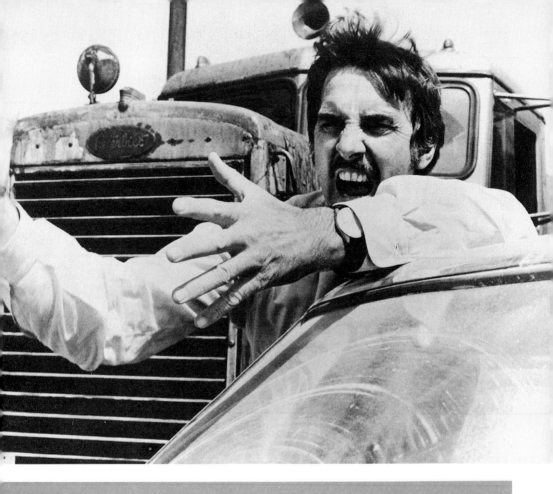

Dennis Weaver, as the suburban travelling salesman being mysteriously menaced by an anonymous truck driver in *Duel*, 1971. Weaver needed some convincing by Spielberg that 'Mr Average' was the right way to play the character of Mann, but his performance helped to make *Duel* one of the most admired TV films of all time. For a change, a TV product was converted into a feature film rather than the other way round.

before, what the film was to be about. It also helped Spielberg to plan his two- and three- camera shots, which covered so much of the road action at the same time that he could make the film in just over two weeks rather than the more usual two months.

The night before each shoot, I'd stake out all my shots. I would literally put stakes in the ground and say 'A, B, and C cameras go here.' The three cameras would be about 100 yards apart. I would simply run the car and then the truck past the cameras, with the fourth camera in the car shooting the truck . . . Then I'd just turn the cameras around and the procession would come right back again.

His childhood experience of filming with limited resources was already beginning to pay dividends. Such careful planning is a Spielberg hallmark that, paradoxically, enables him to prompt improvisations out of his actors. He had first to convince Weaver, who had just started playing television tough-guy *McCloud* after a long career in both film and TV, that his character should be more mild-mannered, more average, than the actor would have liked. The whole point of the Mann character is to identify someone who has been so deadened by suburban life that he is obvious prey for any predators on the open road. Once this had been agreed, said Spielberg:

> I'm almost at my most improvisatory when I've planned most thoroughly, when my story-boards are in continuity. That gives me confidence to ad lib. I sort of lose my confidence when I haven't done my homework, and I haven't planned ahead a number of weeks. I'm basically very loose when it comes to working with actors in a non-logistical setting. But within an action sequence or within a climatic arrangement of scenes, I pretty much stick to what I've visualized months before. Then when I improvise, I improvise around the planned stuff.

Once the filming in Soledad Canyon, California, had stopped, Spielberg had to experience the enormous difficulties of post-production that the scheduling imposed upon him:

> When I made *Duel* I had three weeks from the time I yelled 'Cut, print, that's a wrap!' to the time it was on the air. I had to cut *Duel* down from two and a half hours to 74 minutes; I had four editors working furiously at the same time; I was roller-skating from editing room to editing room; Billy Goldenberg only had a couple of days to write and score the music; I dubbed the whole thing in two days; and then we corrected the colour and it was on TV.

In fact, this experience of having to work at speed was to serve him well; the instinctive rapid editing of *Duel* is one its most successful features. Even so, as a result of this schedule, he vowed that if he ever got back into television (which he did with his *Amazing Stories* 15 years later) he would allow himself and his directors more lead time for their work.

It is a very simple story with very little dialogue and leaves plenty of room for audience speculation about why the truck is behaving as it is. It can be seen variously as a technological western, with the vehicles replacing horses, a psycho-thriller in which we are not quite sure at first whether Mann is actually being persecuted or whether his neuroses and paranoia are getting the better of him, or simply as a David and Goliath tale. All films have to be examined in the context of the time in which they were made, and all three of these themes were major concerns in the America of the late 1960s and early 1970s. The genre of the classic western, for example, was in decline but was being replaced by 'urban westerns' such as *Dirty Harry* (1971) in which the hero was more ambivalent in his philosophy of dealing with the 'bad guys'. *Duel* borrows heavily from both strands; David Mann is hardly a Gary Cooper or John Wayne figure but, once pushed, he is forced to do what a Mann's gotta do. He is a worm that turns, like Jimmy Stewart in *Firecreek* (1967). As in so many of his later films, Spielberg presents an ordinary middle-class suburban hero, someone who does not go looking for trouble but who, when pushed and threatened, can summon up reserves of strength and resourcefulness that can overcome all dangers. Spielberg is not mocking suburbia; he regards it as the American backbone. Yet the desert is hardly the environment David Mann knows best; he is a middle-class suburbanite who is forced to operate in an alien environment for reasons he doesn't understand. On another level it falls into a more classical tradition of someone who has to return to long-forgotten primeval instincts in order to survive, as recognized by Mann at the end of the film as he sits like a caveman against the sunset, almost dehumanized by his ordeal, brooding over the 'corpse' of his adversary.

Of course, the film might not have been consciously intended as any of these things. But Spielberg has said:

> All the symbols others read into *Duel*, I had encountered or anticipated along the way. But in shooting from scene to scene they were not my primary concern. What I was really striving for was a statement about American paranoia. *Duel* was an exercise in paranoia.

'*Duel* is an indictment of machines,' said Spielberg elsewhere, 'and I determined very early on that everything about the film would be the complete disruption of our whole technological society.' People will indeed continue to read all sorts of things into the film that are not there – although only a few eagle-eyed viewers will be able to catch a split-second glimpse of Spielberg himself in the back seat of Mann's vehicle on the large-screen format. This mistake was not even spotted by Spielberg himself while originally editing the film on a small format Moviola device and only became apparent when he saw the larger ratio image not permitted by television. 'But if there's something I hate more than seeing myself in a movie, it's seeing grain on-screen. I just let it go.'

Duel is a day-time nightmare that draws heavily for its suspense on such Hitchcock films as *Psycho*, *North by Northwest* and *The Birds*. A psychopathic techno-killer is on the loose and Mann's realization that he has to face the menace alone is achieved through agonizing monologues with himself. There is the constant danger, because the truck is marked 'flammable', that a collision will result in a huge explosion – which never happens, even at the end; it is Mann's car that blows up – and the tension is sustained by the noise of the motor engines and the trucks bellowing horn. Mann's personal plight is contrasted skilfully with the anonymous and unreasonable truck. Spielberg had not intended initially that the driver's face would ever be seen, but he quickly recognized while filming on the road that the driver's face was being hidden by the giant bulkhead of the truck and by the glare of the sun. He therefore decided to exploit and extend this vital aspect of the film's suspense. From the word go, said Spielberg,

> I wanted the truck to become the personified villain. I wanted the film to begin very slowly with this man pulling out of his middle-class neighbour-hood and driving through the city streets and then on to the open road and the film unwinded rather than happened, it unwinded in such a way that each incident had to be more exciting and more tempting than the one before so that it would snowball into a climax. I wanted the film to be a grim awakening to the man who plays it safe. He leads a normal life, nothing dangerous every happens to him, and then this truck represents all the hidden dangers of life that can happen to a man who isn't aware of his own mortality.

One of Spielberg's heroes, David Lean, recalled that when he first saw *Duel* in Europe, 'immediately I knew that here was a very bright new director. Steven takes real pleasure in the sensuality of forming action scenes – wonderful flowing movements. He has this extraordinary size of vision, a sweep that illuminates his films. But then Steven is the way the movies used to be. He just loves making films. He is entertaining his teenage self – and what is wrong with that?' There followed critical acclaim from the likes of Dilys Powell and awards such as the Special Mention at the 12th Monte Carlo television festival, the Grand Prix of the first French Festival du Cinema Fantastique, the Gariddi d'Oro as the best debut film at the Taormina festival in Italy and the Picture-of-the-Month trophy in West Germany.

In 1973, the film started to attract rave reviews in the United States where it was emerging as a cult movie. In the meantime, *Duel* had brought Spielberg to the attention of producers Richard D. Zanuck and David Brown who wanted him to direct his first feature film proper, *The Sugarland Express*. But before we can take up that story, there is one interesting footnote to the first TV phase of Spielberg's life. If he had stuck to his contract, he may have retained sufficient influence to prevent the chase sequences for *Duel* being chopped up and used for an episode of *The Incredible Hulk* in 1978. Since then, he ensures that film contracts prevent any cannibalization of his work without his prior permission.

THE SUGARLAND EXPRESS (1974)

Inundated with offers following the critical acclaim afforded to *Duel*, Spielberg found none of them to his liking and returned to his television work while developing his own story ideas. One of these, written for a film directed by John Erman and starring Cliff Robertson, entitled *Ace Eli and Roger of the Skies* (1973), was Spielberg's first cinema credit as a writer but one that was notable only for its early indication of Spielberg's love affair with aeroplanes. He also worked for two and a half months on preparing to direct *White Lightning*, starring Burt Reynolds, although he withdrew from that project when he realized that 'it wasn't something that I wanted to do for a first film. I didn't want to start my career as a hard-hat, journeyman director. I wanted to do something that was a little more personal.' Contracted still to Universal, he was ordered to make the television film *Savage* ('the first and last time the studio ordered me to do something'), and made the more satisfying *Something Evil* for CBS.

During this time he rediscovered a newspaper account that he had filed away some time before from the now defunct Los Angeles *Citizen News*. It told the story of a desperate young couple's attempts to rescue their baby from a foster home in Sugarland, Texas. The story appealed to Spielberg because it would allow him to explore some of his central preoccupations, such as parenthood, children separated from their parents, the whole idea of the hunter and the hunted and the role of the media in the contemporary world. Spielberg's script was tightened up by Hal Barwood and Mathew Robbins, two old friends from the University of Southern California (and whom Spielberg would cast as the two missing airmen who step out of the mothership at the end of *Close Encounters of the Third Kind*). He was delighted with their final script and 'I believe I've gotten to the point where I can appreciate a good piece of material and translate it into film without my own ego showing up on the screen'. Zanuck and Brown, now at Universal, were prepared to produce it and had the power to do so since they had recently reunited Newman and Redford for Universal in *The Sting* (1973). The 25-year-old Spielberg was further excited by the prospect of being the first director to be allowed properly to utilize the newly-developed Panaflex 35mm camera on the film that its manufacturer, Panavision, had selected from over 100 requests to put the tiny new camera through its paces.

In contrast to his earlier television work, in which Spielberg experimented with a number of clever or fancy camera shots and angles 'to get it out of my system', he decided on this film that 'the action is the eccentricity'. Almost as if to emphasize the point, he has Lou Jean and Clovis (played by Goldie Hawn and William Atherton) watch a Road Runner cartoon at a drive-in movie theatre. Spielberg and his cinematographer, Vilmos Zsigmond (whose credits included *McCabe and Mrs Miller* – which Spielberg loved – *Deliverance* and *The Long Goodbye*) allowed the camera – even the new Panaflex camera, which allowed for 360° panning shots inside the car – to be 'nothing but a spectator – though Vilmos and I have let the camera editorialize when that's been necessary'. Ironically, it was Spielberg's use of the new camera that caught many critics' attention, although the public appears to have seen merely another car chase-cum-road movie.

There are indeed elements of that genre, epitomized by Carey Loftin's spectacularly staged car crashes and stunts ('America on Wheels', as it

William Atherton, Goldie Hawn and Michael Sacks in *The Sugarland Express*, 1973. Spielberg's first, and perhaps his least well-known, film is in some respects atypical. But the director's interest in families in crisis is much in evidence as is his sure touch when filming action sequences.

was described in one review), but Spielberg does demonstrate additional skill in bringing out the human side to the story. He examines the whole notion of the siege mentality when hostages and captors find points of mutual reference and identification. 'We really see,' said Spielberg, 'that the policeman is really more like the husband than the husband is. It's two men who really began in the same small town and went different ways. One took the road to law and order, the other took a wrong turn in life.'

Spielberg was happy to learn how location shots could be made to work for his filming but he is at his most creative with shots filmed inside the car, designed to draw the audience into the developing relationship taking place therein. Interviewed on the set, producer Richard Zanuck explained that the film was 'the slow evolution of their personalities during a 36-hour period that is really the backbone of the story', an intimate relationship developed against the backdrop of the media circus and the huge police posse. Spielberg explained:

> It was about these two young people who had their baby taken from them and were then pursued across Texas by the entire law enforcement division for some very small, petty crimes. It was a media event that just escalated. In Texas there is a posse theory. If a fellow officer is in trouble, everybody, all of his colleagues, jump into their cars and fall in behind to try and help the guy out. In this case 90 police cars were involved in a bumper to bumper pursuit that was strung out over 150 miles across Texas. And, in the end, they actually hired sharpshooters who killed the young man. In the budget of my picture I could only afford 40 or so, but still people could hardly believe it.

Spielberg's talent is certainly evident, although he was customarily quick to point out the contribution made by the crew and by Zsigmond in particular:

> Vilmos is the only cameraman I know who thinks like me in terms of hiding the zoom. I hate to see unmotivated zoom shots, and I see them so often on TV – *zoom in, zoom out!* Vilmos feels the same way about it so we disguise all our zoom shots. You don't notice that the camera has gone from close to far. By the time you would normally become conscious of the zoom a cut has been made and you are only faintly aware that the scene has assumed a different look.

Zsigmond, who felt that he was working with 'a young director who really wants to do the impossible', said of his experience of Spielberg that he:

is probably the most talented director I've worked with. He's only 25 years old, but he seems to have the experience of a man 40 years old. The way he directs a film makes you think that he must have many features behind him, but this is his first feature and it's really unbelievable. I can only compare him to Orson Welles, who was a very talented director when he was very young. There's one great thing that I like about him very much. Most young directors, when they get their first film, somehow get timid; they pull back; they try to play it safe, because they are afraid that they will never get another chance to make a feature. Not Steve. He really gets right into the middle. He really tried to do the craziest things. Most of the shots he gets he could only dream about doing, up until now. He could never do them on TV . . . Some of the people on the crew may laugh at us when we're going through the rehearsals and all that insanity, but at the end, when we've got it, they seem pleased that we did do something that seemed impossible to do.

Such co-operation between director and cinematographer, with them working together rather than at odds with one another, produced a harmony that was to be recreated on *Close Encounters* several years later.

Although *Sugarland* secured extremely favourable reviews, including that legendary tribute from Pauline Kael, it only fared reasonably well at the box office. Dilys Powell thought it 'generally balanced, accomplished, satisfying' while Richard Schickel in *Time* caught up with her by identifying Spielberg as one to watch. 'It did get good reviews,' said Spielberg, 'but I would have given away all those reviews for a bigger audience. The movie just broke even; it didn't make any money.' He was also pretty angry because the film was not marketed properly; 'people saw that it was Goldie Hawn's film and thought it was small – you know a real teddy bear! Also there was the title; most people thought it was a kid's film.' The film's release, twelve months after it was finished, four months after the enthusiastic previews and 28 mediocre advertising campaign ideas later, clashed with the success of *The Sting* and with other 'road movies', such as *Badlands* and *Thieves Like Us* (neither of which did very well either). Although *Sugarland* did win best screenplay prize for Spielberg, Robbins and Barwood at the 1974 Cannes Film Festival, the film itself made barely $3 million at the box office (although it did, eventually, make a slight profit when it was sold to television).

Spielberg did say years later: 'That's the one film that I can honestly say if I had to do all over again I'd make *Sugarland Express* in a completely different fashion.' He would have made the first half of the film from the police point of view, to build up a more sympathetic picture of the

Captain Tanner character; 'I would never show the fugitive kids, only hear their voices over the police radio, maybe see three heads in the distance through binoculars.' He didn't feel he had been sufficiently sympathetic to the forces of law and order, 'why the posse formed, why there was an overwhelming amount of vigilante activity and freestyle heroism, and why Tanner finally had to make the decision to put an end to this by destroying the characters in the car through force and violence.' As it stands, Tanner's decision 'is for me much too weak and unmotivated' and the portrayal of the young parents too sympathetic, reducing the significance of their criminality – the fact that they were armed, dangerous and holding a hostage. In the second half of the film, he would have brought this out, 'how really naive and backwoodsy and really stupid their goals were . . . I would have then . . . created an understanding of this camaraderie, this triumvirate relationship inside the automobile with the cop becoming nothing less than an accomplice.' Spielberg was to make up for this in his next film, which did explore a triumvirate relationship involving a policeman, not in a car, but on a boat.

JAWS (1975)

Spielberg's second feature film, made at the age of 26, was also produced by Zanuck and Brown, with whom the young director had enjoyed working. He found Peter Benchley's novel in their office – in galley-proofs, two months before it was published – and felt he could do something with it, even though it was hardly a work of great literature but 'an airplane book'. Although both producers knew that *Sugarland* was gaining more critical than box office acclaim, they none the less eventually decided to back the young director to film *Jaws* after discussing the project with him in Europe while Spielberg was publicizing *Duel*. The initial budget was to be $2¼ million

Spielberg had his reservations right from the start, not least because the shark versus man theme was in some ways too similar to his man versus machine story in *Duel*. 'For me,' said Spielberg later, 'the film was necessary. I also wanted to do it for hostile reasons. I read it and felt I had been attacked. It terrified me and I wanted to strike back.' Moreover, 'the book was about something Peter Benchley was interested in [it was written around the time of the Watergate scandal], beyond sharks, while the film is based on subject matter that interests me, beyond sharks.' He did, however, love the final 120 pages 'an amazing set piece, a battle between three men amongst themselves and – in the background – a fish they knew nothing about.' Once the script went from Benchley to

Howard Sackler (author of the play *The Great White Hope* and a fishing expert) and then (apparently) to John Milius and finally to Carl Gottlieb, who was to re-write much of these various versions while shooting, Spielberg was happier because of the input he was then able to get from the actors. He was delighted with the cast that eventually assembled - Robert Shaw, fresh from *The Sting*, instead of Sterling Hayden; Roy Scheider, whose role in *The French Connection* had impressed Spielberg, instead of Charlton Heston – and the young actor who had so impressed him in George Lucas's 1973 hit *American Graffiti*, Richard Dreyfuss (chosen in preference to Timothy Bottoms and Jeff Bridges). These three would enable Spielberg to investigate the theme of paranoia that was already apparent in his earlier film and television work. Shaw, who was to emerge as the film's Captain Ahab shared Spielberg's reservations about the book's quality but, on the advice of his wife and of his secretary, had decided to accept the role in his second Zanuck-Brown film in succession.

Filming at Martha's Vineyard was fraught with unforeseen difficulties. Instead of the original 52-day shooting schedule, the film took three times longer than that to complete because of the difficulties of shooting at sea and because of problems with the three 24-feet, one-and-a-half ton mechanical polyurethane sharks (affectionately nicknamed Bruce) made at a cost of $150,000 each. The first Bruce sank on its first test and the second exploded. Models were mainly used for obvious reasons, although a second unit was dispatched to film live sharks in Australia under the supervision of experts Ron and Valerie Taylor (of *Blue Water, White Death* fame [1971]). There was no way the timid Spielberg was going to use real sharks off Martha's Vineyard. Besides, he recalled:

> I was yelling: Disney! The minute I read the script, I was yelling Disney! We've gotta get the guy who did the squid in *20,000 Leagues Under the Sea!* Whoever he was who did the Disney films, I want him! I didn't know who he was at the time. It turned out to be Bob Mattey and we hired him to build us a shark.

Bad weather, angry locals, labour disputes (and the fact that they were forced to start shooting earlier than they would have wanted by the impending actors' strike), together with Spielberg's need to constantly re-write the script, meant that the budget escalated to well over $6 million and the shooting schedule to 155 days. Spielberg later discovered that the producers had even considered sacking him and abandoning the project. For their part, the actors were conscious of a potential disaster because the film depended not upon their skills but upon the acting abilities of a cross-eyed mechanical model whose jaws would not close

Stars from *Jaws*, 1975: Roy Scheider, Robert Shaw, Richard Dreyfuss and Lorraine Gary (*clockwise from top left*) with the killer shark.

properly (as related by Brian De Palma who visited Spielberg during filming).

As it was, these difficulties produced two factors that greatly helped the final film and its success. First were the extraordinary performances of Shaw, Scheider and Dreyfuss. On this, Spielberg has said:

> When I'm working with a script that I'm not a hundred per cent sanguine about, as I was with *Jaws*, I can be *very* open to suggestion. I think it really helps to sit the actors around a table and talk about the problems of the script. In general, I think actors can contribute much more than ten hours a day of acting. I guess I require writing and inventing services from them at times, too.

The script was accordingly changed virtually every day as a result of their daily rehearsals. 'There were improvisational readings; often I would wake up in the middle of the night and write down some idea and shoot it the next day. A lot of it was free expression.'

The second successful ingredient was Spielberg's decision to hide the shark for as long as possible which, together with the aid of John Williams' outstanding and memorable shark theme, helps to heighten the suspense. As Spielberg said:

> I think a) it's more challenging and more fun to disguise the menace, and b) I think that the collective audience has a better, broader imagination than I do. They fill in the spaces between the lines. They saw a much more horrific shark in their heads when I suggested an occurrence below the surface than I provided with the rubber shark when my commercial sensibilities told me I had to make it visible.

'I wanted the water to mean shark,' he explained. 'The horizon to mean shark. I wanted the shark presence to be felt everywhere before I finally let people get a glimpse of the shark itself.' Spielberg attributed much of this to John Williams' score: 'what he did on *Jaws* was just incredible. His music made it another movie, made it better than I ever thought it could be.'

'What I think I wound up with,' said Spielberg, 'was exactly what I went for.' That, according to Pauline Kael, was a 'cheerfully perverse scare movie'; other critics saw it more in the context of the disaster movie boom of the 1970s. As for Spielberg, who wanted it to be a 'primal scream movie', he said:

> There were certain questions about *Jaws* that had to be answered before the final blows. There was the whole opening and closing of the beaches issue, which became academic once the shark attacked on the Fourth of July. So that paid off. There was more than one climax in *Jaws*. The first act proved it was indeed a shark out there. The second act proved the mayor wrong, the beleagured police chief right. And the third act was basically a man-against-beast tale. It could be called a celebration of man's constant triumph over nature – not necessarily for the good.

Spielberg took an extra six months editing the film with Verna Fields, often returning to her swimming pool to shoot extra scenes. The scene in which Richard Dreyfuss finds the body of a fisherman while diving to look at a wrecked boat was in fact added after the film previewed in Dallas. Spielberg explained:

> I still didn't feel I had enough reaction in the second act of the movie, so I designed the head coming out of the hole in the boat . . . And that became the big scream of the movie. I felt the movie needed an explosive surprise at that point.

Fields, a good friend, was awarded the Oscar for her editing of *Jaws*. But when they saw the final film, the producers and director showed it to Sidney Sheinberg who asked: 'Isn't there any more?' They all feared it would turn out to be 'a shark with turkey feathers' but $410 million dollars later they had changed their mind and someone had painted shark's teeth and added a fin to the giant six-foot plastic red and yellow chicken in Spielberg's office. The film took $60 million in the first month of its American release; Spielberg's earnings were $50,000 – and three per cent of the profits. Within three months, it had become the most successful movie in terms of box-office takings of all time.

Critically, the film earned some comparisons with Hitchcock, although *Time*, in a five-page cover-story, felt that Spielberg's characters 'lack the quirks and little guilts that make Hitchcock's creations stay in the memory'. The film's opening sequence, in which the shark claims its first victim, is perhaps as celebrated a scene as anything Hitchcock ever directed. Without special effects and relying on camera angles and the music of John Williams to create tension Spielberg firmly implants the idea of an unknown assailant of fearsome ferocity into the audience's imagination. *Time's* reviewer none the less admired the young director's technique and concluded that it was a 'very American' film. Frank Rich, who was to join *Time* two years later, in a sense explained what this meant when he wrote that Spielberg was 'blessed with a talent that is absurdly absent from most American filmmakers these days; this man actually knows how to tell a story on-screen.' Other reviewers praised the film for its ability to combine horror and suspense with the themes of small-town politics and man against nature. As usual, Spielberg proves to be the best analyst of his own work:

> The film hit a nerve somewhere. Maybe because it is basically Freudian. We've been taught to suppress our fears – the macho cover – but *Jaws* makes it safe to express fear in public. Then there's the theory of its relationship to our pre-natal hours, because people are like little sharks at one point. They know how to survive in water for a while. Also the film illustrates that Common Man can become a hero by dealing with . . . what has to be dealt with.

Ironically, the film's financial success soon began to produce a critical backlash against Spielberg, reflected at the Oscars (although it was nominated in four categories, including Best Picture), and subsequent rumours of disenchantment amongst the crew made Spielberg disinclined to have anything to do with the inevitable sequels that Universal Studios was already planning. The experience of filming the original was bad enough: 'I still have dreams that I'm trying to finish that picture.' This was just as well, given that perhaps the most memorable aspect of those sequels were the kind of skilful advertising poster captions that *Sugarland Express* could well have benefited from.

The success of *Jaws* could have turned the young man's head but, said the producer of his next film, 'all it did was give him more toys to play with. The interesting thing now is that he's still maturing as a person. He's mastered his craft. I think his films will change now as his experience deepens. In other words, he's only going to get better.' As for Spielberg himself, the bad memories of making the film combined with a realization that it had really come more from the head rather than the heart:

> Sure, I tend to gravitate towards things I think I can do well. Shock-value films. But I'm not very violent, you know. I pretty much knew what *Jaws* would do to an audience. It was an experiment in terror. It was a nightmare to shoot. I didn't have any fun making it. But I had a *great* time planning it, going tee-hee-hee!

CLOSE ENCOUNTERS OF THE THIRD KIND (1977)

After *Jaws*, Spielberg talked of making a film called Bingo Long (eventually made in 1976 by John Badham for Universal as *The Bingo Long Travelling All Stars and Motor Kings*), a story of a travelling black baseball team in the 1930s. He has never yet made a film about his beloved sport although he was to return to his interest in making a film about black Americans with *The Color Purple*. For the moment the opportunity emerged to make another film about a subject for which he had long nurtured a fascination and a passionate interest. This really was to be one from the heart.

After the success of *Jaws*, Spielberg was able to make just about any film he wanted to and he had been thinking about a UFO film for some time. He had in fact raised the idea with the producers, Michael and Julia Phillips, before even *Sugarland Express*. Digging back to his most ambitious teenage film, *Firelight*, and to a story he had written in 1970 entitled 'Experiences', he decided to take two years writing and making *Close Encounters*. Its original working title was 'Watch the Skies', taken from the last line of 1951 science fiction classic *The Thing from Another Planet*. *Firelight*, an 8mm-film about scientists investigating mysterious lights in the sky and hostile alien invaders, had cost the 16-year-old Spielberg $500 to make. *Close Encounters* was to be different. Columbia were persuaded to take on the project for $8 million. The budget was eventually to reach $20 million.

Essentially it is a fictional account of various reports of UFO sightings woven together into a single story. An encounter of the first kind is a UFO sighting; the second kind is direct physical evidence of a UFO; the third kind is an encounter between humans and aliens. 'It's science fiction if you don't believe, and fact if you do. For me it's speculation,' said Spielberg.

Dr J. Allen Hyneck, an astronomer who served as consultant to the US Air Force on UFO sightings, was brought in as technical adviser for the film. He said that 'even though the film is fiction, it's based for the most part on the known facts of the UFO mystery, and it certainly catches the flavour of the phenomenon.' Hyneck was an interesting choice. He had been employed by the US Government as a sceptic, the man who would find rational explanations to dismiss the phenomena. As he investigated

Producer, Julia Phillips, UFO expert and technical consultant, Dr J Allen Hynek and Director, Steven Spielberg during the filming of *Close Encounters of the Third Kind* in 1977.

more and more incidents he discovered that there were some that could not be easily dismissed. When he reported his findings he was told just to get on with the job he had been appointed to do, whereupon he resigned and wrote a book attacking the Air Force. According to Spielberg: 'I met Hyneck because he was a man who had suddenly learned to believe, and that was a very uncommon thing to do.'

Spielberg encountered opposition from the Air Force and the Army and so when it was necessary to shoot scenes involving the military he had to do it 'the old-fashioned way' with army suits from the costume store. Spielberg said:

> I really found my faith when I heard that the Government was opposed to the film. If NASA took the time to write me a 20-page letter, then I knew there must be something happening. I had wanted cooperation from them, but when they read the script they got very angry and felt that it was a film that would be dangerous. I felt they mainly wrote the letter because *Jaws* convinced so many people around the world that there were sharks in toilets and bathtubs, not just in the oceans and rivers. They were also afraid the same kind of epidemic would happen with UFOs.

The appointment of Douglas Trumbull, the man who devised the special effects for Kubrick's *2001: A Space Odyssey*, and Vilmos Zsigmond, whose camera style of heightened naturalism had been evident on *The Sugarland Express*, indicated that Spielberg was up to something different. The entire project was shrouded in such secrecy prior to the film's release that the crew nicknamed it 'No Encounters of the Publicity Kind'. 'I wanted to surprise,' Spielberg said. 'And the only way in the world you're going to do that is by keeping quiet about what's in it.'

Paul Schrader had a go at the script but Spielberg didn't like it, creating not a little acrimony between the two men. He decided to write it himself.

> The only reason that I wrote *Close Encounters* was that I couldn't find anybody who would write it the way I wanted it . . . It was either all family or all UFOs. Nobody wanted to do both.

He researched the phenomenon of UFOs by reading old copies of Life magazine, reading published accounts of UFO sightings, talking to scientists, pilots and air traffic controllers and 'even four security people at the Pentagon who, during the early 1950s, had worked in the intelligence corps and were around when UFOs buzzed the capital; there was a great flap in Washington. It sounds like a great science fiction film, but Washington took it very seriously.' But the 'best part of the research' was conversations with 'average family types who never expect anything extraordinary to happen until it actually does . . . because it supported my feeling about the first two-thirds of the film. The last part is just my vision, my hope and philosophy.' Spielberg had long pondered the wonders of outer space, from that evening when he was six when his father drove him out to see a meteor storm. 'But I'm never really thinking about outer space in outer space.' Talking about the toy-cluttered set created to represent the Neary home Spielberg said that he was attempting 'to create some kind of reality against which people would consider the fantasy of the first encounter'. He explained further:

> I love juxtaposing, you know, the cosmos with a real sort of suburban reality. I love anything that is contrary to what we're used to. And it's essential for a film of this kind to base it here, on Earth. It's taking place in your backyard. You really have to believe in Earth before you can believe in flying saucers.

Having finished the screenplay and story-boarded his ideas, he brought in Joe Alves, with whom he had worked on both *Sugarland* and *Jaws*, as production designer. 'The two of us occupied a boxcar bungalow on the sidelot of the Burbank Studios for over a year. There we drew little pictures in charcoal, pencil and crayon of extra-terrestrial concepts, UFOs and landing sites.' While an artist (George Jensen) painted up the ideas and while Alves was scouring America for suitable locations, Spielberg approached Trumbull, who loved the script and liked Spielberg.

> Doug looked at the paintings, scratched his head and said he'd do his best. You see I had no idea how to engineer the things I had in my head. He built some machines, hired the best people, and began showing me tests. They absolutely adhered to the original concept.

Because that concept required an area larger than any soundstage in the world, Spielberg had to use a huge World War Two dirigible hanger in Mobile, Alabama. Alves converted the 450×250×90-foot hangar into a soundstage six times larger than any available to make it appear like Indiana at night. Filming took place between May and September 1976 with Vilmos Zsigmond as director of photography.

When Spielberg wanted extra scenes shot Zsigmond was unavailable and so he subsequently employed Bill Fraker, John Alonzo, Laszlo Kovaks and Douglas Slocombe at various points over the following months. They are all great friends and knew each others styles intimately and because they all looked at what had already been filmed before shooting new scenes it is virtually impossible to identify which scenes were shot by whom. The sequence in which Lacombe arrives in Northern

India as a huge crowd is chanting the Sky Tones was filmed by Slocombe in January 1977. This Indian location, employing 3,500 extras to point skywards, was to have been the final shooting on the film, following the move from Mobile to Devil's Tower, Wyoming, but characteristically Spielberg thought of some extra scenes. They included one in which a team of UN investigators discovers a stranded ship in the middle of the desert. This scene was filmed in the Mojave Desert by Bill Fraker in May 1977. According to Spielberg, Bill Fraker 'had the kind of wonderful ideas I'm not about to pass up.' This scene was, in fact, only used in the Special Edition, released in 1980. The Special Edition is, in fact, three minutes shorter than the original film and contains such minute changes that it is barely possible to tell which scenes have been changed. One of the main additions was the footage showing the entry of Neary into the mothership at the end.

The mothership itself, a gigantic 'city of lights' as Spielberg asked Carlo Rambaldi to design it, appeared to dwarf the mountain in the movie. In fact it was six foot in diameter, a 40-pound plexiglass, steel plywood and fibreglass model built by Greg Jein. The informed eye can spot various jokey references stuck to the supposedly quarter mile wide ship – a Volkswagen van, a replica of Darth Vader's ship from *Star Wars*, and an upside down R2-D2 from the same film among them.

The use of the famous French film director François Truffaut to play the part of Lacombe, the first time that he had acted in a film not his own, was audacious and ingenious. While he was writing the script, Spielberg felt that Lacombe's part bore a similarity to Truffaut's role in *The Wild Child* (1970). 'I wanted a man-child,' said Spielberg, 'ingenious and wise, a father-figure with this very wide-eyed young outlook on life. I didn't want the stoic with the white hair and pipe. I wanted somebody who could be out in the field, going from country to country, doing his research.' He finally got up the courage to telephone Truffaut in Paris and found him 'quite open to the idea.' Although he had not seen *Jaws*, Truffaut had seen and greatly admired *Duel*. Besides, because he was writing a book on actors and acting, he welcomed the idea of working as an actor in another director's film 'as a kind of laboratory experience'. Though initially intimidated by the idea of having to direct a man whose films he greatly admired, Spielberg did in fact find Truffaut easier to direct than the other actors because, as a director, he instinctively knew when Spielberg was unhappy with a take. 'I could never relate to François on a director-actor relationship; it was always a director to director about an actor relationship . . . he is used to small, personal crews and cast; low budgets. When he came on the set it was the first time he had seen the old Hollywood being run by the new.' Using a

Francois Truffaut and Richard Dreyfuss in *Close Encounters of the Third Kind*, 1977.

Frenchman who has mostly to communicate through an interpreter (played by Bob Balaban) is a nice touch by Spielberg in a film where communication is a central motif. With communication as a central theme of the film, Truffaut and Dreyfuss bury their differences to team up in the common goal of understanding what the visitors from another planet and culture are trying to say.

As with *Jaws*, John Williams' score is essential to the film. Even before he wrote the score for *Jaws* we were having meetings about *Close Encounters*. We're very close friends, and I'm so involved with music anyway. I wanted more of a mathematical, musical communication than a 'Take me to your leader'.

Talking about the scene in which the mothership communicates with the Earth computers by means of a musical dialogue Spielberg said:

I don't have all the answers, and I didn't want to pretend that I knew the answers. There were questions that needed answering. How does the music translate into English? During the musical exchange, what are they saying to one another? . . . I'm happy to know that they said hello. It's a movie for people who like to use their imagination.

In *Close Encounters* Spielberg demonstrated one of his greatest talents: the direction of children. He gets an extraordinary performance out of Cary Guffey. He achieved this

by adopting him; we were inseparable for three months. I knew what he liked and what he didn't, and how to get him to smile. I would describe what he was reacting to and he would make pictures from my words and react to those pictures. He was an extraordinary kid and, for a three-year-old, very bright.

The aliens were played by 50 six- and seven-year-old children. Spielberg often had to jokingly shout on the set: 'ETs! Stop fooling around!' Truffaut, himself a talented director of children, 'adopted' the lead creature. 'You'd find him standing there talking to this inanimate object in French.' The scene with the aliens was in fact filmed six stops overexposed, a bold but inspired method of making the incredible seem more plausible. 'The lighting 'saved my ass on the aliens', said Spielberg. 'I wanted you to have to strain your eyes through the light to interpret what was on the screen.' The result is warmth, not a stark historic meeting but a warm embrace.

The religious symbolism that many analysts have seen in Spielberg's work, particularly in *Close Encounters*, has produced almost as many good moments as the films themselves. For example, one writer has stated:

In a famous essay, 'The UFO as a religious symbol', C.G. Jung suggested that modern man appropriates machine images to his own magical purposes, and turns the stuff of science to myth and religion. No filmmaker does this better than Steven Spielberg, a suburban animist with a tinge of Manicheanism.

Pauline Kael at least put her religious interpretation in plain English. 'God is up there in a crystal chandelier spaceship and he likes us.' It is certainly true that, as Spielberg himself admitted, the last half-hour of the film 'is all phantasmagoria, in which the movie practically becomes another movie' and that all sorts of religious interpretations are possible. But Spielberg is merely teasing those who wish to read such matters into the film. It really owes more to Spielberg's own memories, experiences and fantasies.

The release of *Star Wars*, six months before CE3K (as it came to be known) knocked *Jaws* off the Number One all-time spot, but George Lucas's success proved to be the best possible way of whetting audience appetites for another science fiction movie. Frank Rich, an early fan of Spielberg's and an influential critic with Time (which had helped to finance the movie), wrote of 'the breathless wonder which the director brings into every frame . . . The freshness of the vision is contagious – and exhilarating . . . almost childlike. *Close Encounters* is part of a celebration of innocence.' Veteran science fiction writer Ray Bradbury was ecstatic about the film, describing it as 'THE film we've all been waiting for':

> In fact, we were waiting for it before we were born. The ghost in us, the secret stuffs of genetics, was waiting. The Life Force was waiting, waiting to be born, waiting to be called forth. Close Encounters called. We feel ourselves being born, truly, for the first time.

Despite such a rapturous reception, however, *Close Encounters* took only two Oscars, although Spielberg was nominated for an Oscar as Best Director, (*Star Wars* took seven). John Williams won the Best Musical Score Oscar for *Star Wars* rather than CE3K and Richard Dreyfuss won the Best Actor award for *The Goodbye Girl*.

3

Spielberg and the American Past

The most expensive habit in the world is celluloid, not heroin, and I need a fix every few years. People want to see pictures that are 99.9% escapist. They're demanding more on-screen than ever before. The drawback of expensive movies is not the guilt so much as how much you have to make to earn a profit . . . There comes a point when there just aren't that many people in the world going to movies. There is a ceiling. There *is* a limit.

Although many of Spielberg's films possess a timeless quality, most are firmly rooted in a particular period of time. As a man with deep feeling for the culture of which he is a part, its past, present and future, he has chosen to set several of his films firmly in periods of American history that have helped to shape the American consciousness and the world into which he was born. As a myth-maker himself, and as a man whose very business is myth-making, he also seems fascinated more by the way the past is regarded by the present or the way in which the past was mirrored by movies than by the very serious historical issues that form the backdrop of his movies. Whether it be Indiana Jones fighting Nazis (and even meeting Hitler himself in *The Last Crusade*) or John Belushi repelling Japanese invaders of Los Angeles in *1941*, the overriding approach of Spielberg to these topics is his sense of fun. As he said of *1941*:

Well, we're taking history and bending it like a pretzel. I've taken this pillar of truth and *shredded* it into a movie that is visually madcap and quite nuts . . . Hypertension is fun!.

However, in *Poltergeist* he does make the more serious point of warning of the dangers of trying to build a modern lifestyle over a graveyard in disregard of the past, with bodies emerging in the swimming pool in the final scenes to take their revenge on suburbia. Such references in fact reflect Spielberg's preoccupation with his own past. It is one way he rationalizes his own place in the great order of things, by taking command of a world in which he, like virtually everyone else, is a victim of events beyond his control. In this respect the rapid action of his films not only reflects his television experience but also the quickened pace of modern society. Film puts him back in control of the uncontrollable. Hence his preoccupation with creating order out of chaos, although many felt that his first excursion into full blown comedy left him well and truly out of control.

1941 (1979)

Considered by many to be Spielberg's biggest disaster, *1941* is in fact a fast-moving pyrotechnical comedy with many wonderful moments and improves with subsequent viewing, rather like *The Blues Brothers*, in which Spielberg made another of his rare screen appearances (as the clerk who receives Aykroyd and Belushi's money at the end of the film). Spielberg was nervous about the project throughout shooting: 'Comedy is not my forte. I don't know how this movie will come out. And yes, I'm scared! I'm like the cowardly lion and two successes back to back have not strengthened my belief in my ability to deliver.' Although Spielberg was being unduly modest about his capacity to film comedy – his other films contain many wonderful comic touches – *1941* is really more farce than comedy, owing more to *Hellzapoppin* (1941) and the Keystone Cops than anything else. 'It is a comedy, not a war picture,' he said. It is certainly in keeping with other established Spielberg interests: how ordinary people cope with extraordinary events; paranoia; man versus machine – and so on. 'Whatever it is,' said Spielberg, 'it's the craziest son-of-a-bitch film I've ever been involved with and it's a real risk for me because it's not the linear story form that I'm used to working with.' This format makes it difficult to summarize, and indeed Spielberg was highly conscious of the difficulties of the first half hour of the film in which the principal characters have to be introduced to the audience before the action begins and the characters start interconnecting.

Written by Bob Gale and Robert Zemeckis, *1941* was originally to be directed by John Milius but Spielberg took over when the latter began directing *Big Wednesday* (1978). He had read the script while making *Close Encounters* 'and I just laughed myself sick'. Perhaps he should have left it at that, but his determination to visualize on film what was obviously funny on paper meant that for once his instincts failed him.

1941 was not a year that even young Americans could treat lightly. True, Mel Brooks had poked fun at that most hallowed of American film institutions, the Western, in *Blazing Saddles* (1974) and College America was currently revelling in the National Lampoon phase launched by *Animal House* (1978). But perhaps it was too soon after defeat in one war to lampoon the lunacies of a previous one which began for the USA with another disaster in the Pacific at Pearl Harbor. And despite Spielberg's declared determination not to cater to audience tastes, here he was trying to ride one. He would have done better to do what he had already proven he could do best, namely to rely on his instincts and make his own films regardless of phases. He is, after all, better at anticipating rather than exploiting national mood swings. But then again, he did feel the need at some point to say farewell to his adolescence.

Spielberg had already decided to produce the two Bobs' first film, *I Wanna Hold Your Hand*, and he spent eight weeks with them fine-tuning their latest script through its two working titles of 'Hollywood '41' and 'The Rising Sun'. George Jensen, was recruited again to sketch the story-boards for the entire movie: 'everything was pre-planned in the greatest detail'. Greg Jein was asked to work his miracles on a miniature Los Angeles for the spectacular finale. Cinematographer Bill Fraker started filming the miniatures first and, six months later, the cast and the rest of the crew were assembled, all good friends. Spielberg simply allows them to have a good time with a $28 million budget. The film admittedly can appear to be a group of self-indulgent people playing with the humour that appeals to them most – but then *Monty Python's Flying Circus* did the same thing (or perhaps the Carry On films would be a better British analogy). Spielberg was merely assembling the American equivalent, drawn from the *National Lampoon* and *Saturday Night Live* stables of American humour (the cast also includes small cameo parts for directors Sam Fuller and John Landis, not to mention it being Mickey Rourke's screen debut). It is in this respect an American satirical farce, compressing the experience of seven sets of characters into three separate wartime events – the sighting of a Japanese submarine off the coast of Santa Barbara in 1942, the 'Great Los Angeles Air Raid Panic' that followed, and the fights caused by tension between enlisted men and the unenlisted 'zoot suiters'. All the action takes place in a single night. It was, said Spielberg,

> When we all lost our minds, thought we were being invaded by Japanese commandos, spent every last bullet shooting at clouds for eight hours straight. It's much like the Orson Welles broadcast of *The War of the Worlds* in 1938, except it really happened in Los Angeles.

Spielberg directing in *1941*, 1979. Richard Combs said of this film: 'Its sheer relentless physicality, its elaborately orchestrated pointlessness on every other level, make it probably the purest demonstration of what it means to have two of the all-time commercial block-busters to one's record and one's hands firmly on the fantasy machine.' The film could bear a re-appraisal.

In short it is again about one of Spielberg's favourite subjects: paranoia. The problem was that his own paranoia about making something so different from what he was used to meant that he tended to rely more on the comedians for the comedy rather than on his own proven story-telling abilities.

There are a series of jokes and gags, which Spielberg directs brilliantly as individual scenes, but which don't always string together to form a satisfying whole for some people. 'Yes, there are elements of [*It's a*] "*Mad, Mad [Mad, Mad] World* [1963] and perhaps a few elements of *The*

Russians Are Coming, The Russians are Coming [1966],' said Spielberg, 'but more than anything there are elements of *Hellzapoppin* and that kind of freestyle, madcap comedy.'

Individual incompetence is the essence of a farce about absurd behaviour that results in a collective positive result: the repulsion of the enemy submarine. But this is achieved more by individual accident than by collective design: 'It's going to be a long war' is the final line. Essentially the film is about a group of incompetent but earnest soldiers (led by Dan Aykroyd and including Treat Williams and John Candy) who attempt to protect Los Angeles from a surprise Japanase attack. There are some wonderful jokes along the way in *1941*. At the start of the film, Aykroyd's team is being served in a diner by a teenage kid, Wally (Bobby Di Cicco), who is more preoccupied with winning a dance competition than with the aftermath of Pearl Harbor. The Treat Williams character (Stretch) resents these priorities, which causes a marvellously choreographed slapstick scene, ending with Aykroyd giving the kid a tip: 'Get rid of that shirt; it's in bad taste.' At the airbase, when Donna starts drooling over a B17 bomber, Captain Birkhead starts talking to her about the plane's ability, how it can 'stay up for a long time', that it is built firm and solid because of its tremendous 'forward thrust'. When Ned Beatty's wife (Lorraine Gary, fresh from *Jaws II* [1978]) first explains that she will not have guns in the house, the barrel of Aykroyd's 40mm anti-aircraft cannon crashes through the front door and John Candy knocks as the door falls on top of her. When the Japanese crew capture Slim Pickens and his 1930s radio set, which they cannot get through the hatch, one of them says 'We've got to figure out a way to make these things smaller.' At the dance competition there is a chase sequence between Wally and Stretch that breaks out into a brilliantly choreographed mass fight that spills out into the street. It is an action-packed combination, perhaps the best in the film, drawing upon such varied sources as the music from *The Quiet Man*, saloon fight sequences from Westerns, inter-services fights *From Here to Eternity*, *Keystone Cops* and *Saturday Night Fever*. Meanwhile, while General Stillwell is crying his eyes out in *Dumbo* and singing along with 'When I see an elephant fly', Captain Birkhead and Nancy Allen have gone off to find some aeroplanes from Warren Oates ('the most paranoid colonel you will ever meet in a film' said Spielberg) who gets his men to test whether they are really Japanese invaders on stilts by kicking Birkhead in the shins. The same man mistakenly tries the same trick on Kelso. And the self-parody continues with a Spielberg look-alike dummy operated by Eddie Deezen (himself the image which Spielberg has of himself as a youth) in the giant Ferris wheel.

Having assembled such a talented cast and crew (including many of his

CE3K special effects people), what went wrong? Spielberg's own view was:

> It was quite an experience for me and a quite unlikely choice after making a science-speculative film like *Close Encounters* or a sheer audience horror film like *Jaws*. I had always wanted to try a visual comedy, but with enough adventure and action where I felt that I'd be sort of in my own element and not out in the cold, although there is nothing harder to accomplish than getting an audience to laugh. Getting an audience to scream at a shark or getting an audience to cry at the awesome wonders of outer space and some sort of extra-terrestrial rival is nothing compared to getting 800 people per screening to laugh out loud at something you think is funny. The sense of humour is so subjective and there is nothing more disappointing than expecting a laugh and not getting it – and nothing more rewarding than getting the laughs where you hoped you would.

Part of the problem was that the film was too long, at just under two hours. At the preview screenings in Denver and Dallas, Spielberg became alarmed at audience silences where there should have been laughter and responded by trimming the film, as one reviewer put it, 'too close to the bone'. The result is that the special effects seem to take control of the film, losing the comic impact of many of the characters, who now appear as strangers since there are too many to provide real audience identification. Moreover, they appear to be trying too hard to be funny, rather than playing it straight. Spielberg had also become fascinated by the capacity of the new Louma crane to take his camera where no camera had gone before and he is accordingly a little over-indulgent when experimenting with his new toy, although he did demonstrate just how it could be used beyond that already shown in *Superman* (1978) and *Moonraker* (1979). 'I'm very demanding when it comes to filling the frame and composing it nicely and found that, with the 15-foot arm on the Louma crane, I could fish for the right shot by looking at the monitor and I could get just the shot I wanted.'

Spielberg also seems to have got carried away, egged on by his zany friends, with making the film on studio lots that had served so many of his favourite films. He was revelling in a Hollywood studio tradition of filmmaking that no longer existed (the submarine, for example was shot in the same MGM tank used by Esther Williams for her 1944 underwater extravaganza, *Bathing Beauty*). Untypically for him, he abandoned his story-board just too many times and got carried away by expensive improvisations, not by the characters but by the action. He admitted that 'if I'd shot the picture on location, the film might have been less theatrical and, perhaps, a little more realistic. But I think all of us were after a kind of surrealism. A comedy surrealism.' Some of the jokes are fine and the smoke-filled sets do provide what has been described as 'a dreamlike atmosphere generated by Spielberg's amazingly complex and inventive staging'. But the overall result is that the sum of the many enjoyable parts does not add up to a satisfying whole.

As a result, the film failed to reach audiences in anything like the same way as *Close Encounters* had done. One theory was that audiences reacted with hostility 'at a time of deepening recession' and were 'quite obviously outraged at the waste and extravagance and wanton destruction'. If so, then it was a tribute to the authenticity of the miniatures employed in the film. In America itself, the film was released at the time of a presidential campaign and of the Iranian hostages crisis. It was also beginning to come to terms with defeat in Vietnam and needed no reminder of the bizarre behaviour of its citizens in wartime. Many simply saw it as a bad film and continue to see it as Spielberg's worst. Audiences shunned *1941* in favour of *Star Trek – The Motion Picture* and then *The Empire Strikes Back* – escapist films that boldly took them to galaxies far, far away rather than to planet Earth's bizarre past behaviour. Box office figures were not helped by the critical hostility that greeted the film's release in December 1979. After *Jaws* and *CE3K*, it is likely that certain critics were just waiting for the first sign of weakness and they revelled in finding more than one in the wonderboy's fourth cinema release.

But in reality, as the critic Veronica Geng has pointed out, Spielberg is in fact 'aesthetically the least wasteful, the most economical of directors. He's a recycler. His movies are 100 per cent efficient'. And David Denby in the *New York* magazine, which had predicted *CE3K* would be a flop, this time came to Spielberg's defence:

> He's made a celebration of the gung-ho silliness of old war movies, a celebration of the Betty Grable-Betty Hutton period of American pop culture. In this movie, America is still a very young country – foolish, violent, casually destructive, but not venal. That we joke about a moment of national crisis shows that we are still young – and sane.

Herein, perhaps lies a clue. Spielberg may have been entertaining his teenage self in the film, but America no longer wanted to be seen as immature or naive. Holding American hostages against their will at a time when the Russians really did appear to be coming up fast with their invasion of Afghanistan called for a more serious image of Americans than that presented by the film. Those audiences who refused to pay to see the film were shortly to demonstrate at the ballot box what kind of image they wanted America to project, and elected a movie star from the time of *1941* to do it for them.

THE INDIANA JONES TRILOGY

Raiders of the Lost Ark (1981)

In May 1977, Spielberg was recovering from making *Close Encounters* (still six months away from its release date) by vacationing in Hawaii with George Lucas, who was in turn nervously awaiting the impending opening of *Star Wars*. Together they came up with the idea of a movie, in Lucas' words, 'based on the serials I loved when I was a kid: action movies set in exotic locales with a cliffhanger every second. I wondered why they didn't make movies like that anymore. I still wanted to see them.' So did Spielberg, since he too had loved the *Masked Marvel-Commander Cody* type of stories 'of narrow misses and close calls'. Apart from the Bond films, which were anyway too *British* for these quintessentially American filmmakers, they were starved of the kind of films that as children had made them want to be film directors. So they decided to combine their formidable talents and try to revive the genre for themselves, in the style of the B-movie adventure stories of the 1930s and 1940s executively.

While Spielberg threw himself into producing *Used Cars* and *Continental Divide*, Lucas went ahead with Philip Kaufman in planning the first adventure of their intrepid adventurer, Indiana Jones (whose original name was to be Smith). In his biography of George Lucas (*Skywalking*), Dale Pollock wrote:

> Spielberg wanted *Raiders* to be the movie equivalent of a ride at Disneyland, inexpensive but believable. Lucas wanted it to remain true to the 1930s serials, with gruff dialogue, plenty of action, and cheap sets. As with *Star Wars*, Lucas insisted that *Raiders* be played straight – the characters and situations were not to be mocked. The audience had to laugh with the picture, not at it.

Lucas had clearly put his finger on the root cause of *1941*'s failure but because he was already planning a *Star Wars* sequel, he asked Spielberg to direct and as they had both been impressed by the screenplay of *Continental Divide* (only his second) they brought in its author, Lawrence Kasdan, to work up their ideas from December 1979 onwards. The collaboration between three such fertile minds was to be a hallmark of the film, with all sorts of new ideas being constantly injected as they began filming in June 1980. Even so, true to form, Spielberg story-boarded about 80 per cent of the film in advance (about 6000 images) and kept to about 60 per cent of that, which in turn helped him to bring in the film well under budget and ahead of schedule. 'It's hard to spend your friend's money,' said Spielberg.

The money question was of particular concern to Spielberg following his big budget productions and the *1941* episode. He wanted to help reverse a trend in big-budget Hollywood productions that he himself recognized he had helped to create:

> I went back and looked at my favourite films from the 1930s and 1940s and thought how quickly and cheaply they were made. I think I'm basically a reincarnated director from the 1930s. *Raiders* owes a lot to the Tarzan books, the Amazing Adventures, the pre-comic book books of that era. It was a kind of 'whizz-bang' time.

It might now appear difficult to understand, but Lucas and Spielberg did have some difficulty persuading a major studio to take on the film (but then again, all had rejected the *Star Wars* script). Paramount eventually took on the film with strict penalties if they went over their generous $40 million budget and their 87-day shooting schedule. With their minds duly concentrated, the film was in fact shot in only 73 days – 'the fastest I've ever shot next to my experience on television'. Despite its locations in London, France, Tunisia and Hawaii, they also came in at half the proposed budget with an eventual cost of $20 million. This was achieved by Lucas keeping Spielberg firmly under control (he knew that Spielberg had gone well over-budget in his previous three films), sticking to 60 scenes, each two pages long, revolving around six major dramatic situations. Only later did they reap the rewards of having negotiated the largest ever profit margin ever agreed by a Hollywood studio.

Although the film's strength lies in its action, the 'Lucasberger' (as their collaboration had been dubbed) might have had to pay those penalties if it had not been for the way in which Harrison Ford made the character of Indiana Jones his own (the original choice was for Tom Selleck, who actually auditioned and got the part only to be refused leave of absence from CBS who were launching the *Magnum P.I.* television series at the time). Spielberg had enjoyed Ford's portrayal of Han Solo in *Star Wars*, and of his Indy interpretation he has said of him: 'He's a remarkable combination of Errol Flynn from *The Adventures of Don Juan* and Humphrey Bogart as Fred C. Dobbs in *The Treasure of the Sierra Madre* . . . villainous and romantic all at once.' Also, because of the actors' strike (which ironically prevented the *Magnum* series' launch because it was being filmed in Hawaii), they were lucky to have scheduled the film to be made in Britain where Lucas had had such success with making *Star Wars*. It was there, the home of repertory

Harrison Ford as Indiana Jones in *Raiders of the Lost Ark*, 1981.

theatre, that they picked up the support cast so essential to a successful production, including Denholm Elliot, Paul Freeman, Ronald Lacey and John Rhys-Davies. British cinematographer Douglas Slocombe (who had filmed the India sequences for *CE3K*) and production designer Norman Reynolds were added to the trusted American crew-members of Michael Kahn (as editor) and the young Kathleen Kennedy (as Spielberg's assistant).

The breathtaking opening sequence, which appears to be the end of a previous adventure, was all Lucas's idea (as was the idea of setting it as if in the middle of an on-going adventure, as he did with the Star Wars trilogy). We are immediately plunged into an adventure story of a type almost forgotten in Hollywood. It is a breathless opening. The idea of showing a climax at the start of the film with such pace and skill was quite deliberate. 'George designed that as a glorious tease . . . to let you almost leave the theatre in the first 12 minutes – totally satisfied!' In fact, this entire opening sequence has nothing to do with the film's real plot. What it does is to introduce the character of Indiana Jones, an old-fashioned adventurer, complete with the requisite superhuman athletic skills and courage, but with very real human fears and frailties as well.

There are various tributes in the film to movie adventure stories of the past. As Indiana's plane flies to Egypt a map with a red line moving across it is superimposed over the image, a device used in, amongst other films, *Casablanca*. This scene was, according to Tony Crawley, rented from the 1973 film *The Lost Horizon* to save costs. (Later in the film there is a street scene supposedly taken from *The Hindenburg* [1975], although Richard Edlund maintained that it was shot with miniatures.) Another small tribute to *Casablanca* comes when a distraught Indiana Jones emulates Bogart's Rick drinking following Marion's kidnapping. Ironically, Harrison Ford admitted to never having seen *Casablanca* – but Spielberg had. Ford described *Raiders* as a film that was 'really about movies more than it's about anything else. It's intricately designed as a real tribute to the craft.'

In one of the film's most famous sequences Indiana confronts a sword-wielding Arabian warrior dressed in magnificent black robes and turban in the manner of Omar Sharif in David Lean's *Lawrence of Arabia*. (This was a film much admired by Spielberg who partly-financed its restoration in 1989.) This was originally intended to be a major showdown in the film – 'the most definitive whip versus sword fight in cinematic history'. However, by the time the scene was to be filmed both Harrison Ford and Spielberg were so exhausted by the heat of the Tunisian location and, in Ford's case, gastro-enteritus (Spielberg took his own food with him) that they agreed that Indiana should just shoot the swordsman with his pistol. It is one of the film's most amusing and enduring scenes. It was also one that excited some fanciful, almost conspiratorial, interpretations. Coming so soon after the freeing of the American hostages in Tehran, Indiana's adversary was seen as the stereotypical hated Arab. Some American audiences reacted euphorically to Indiana's instant solution to his problem. 'Reaganism had its first explicit filmic representation,' one scholar wrote.

Paramount discovered that its return to the great adventure films of the past earned just under $225 million. Ten years later Spielberg admitted that *Raiders* was not a particularly deep film:

> . . . it's only a movie . . . not a statement of the times, the way things were in 1936. It takes all the license of an exotic entertainment that aims to thrill and scare and strike one with a sense of wonder – with the cleverness of the hero pitted against an enemy of despicable class and wit. A gravy train movie!

Raiders is perhaps Spielberg's most anonymous movie in terms of being able to see much of the man, rather than his interests outside of movies, in it. 'Raiders was popcorn, but great popcorn.' His next project, *ET*, would be much more personal (*see* Chapter 4).

Indiana Jones and the Temple of Doom (1984)

It had always been intended to make a sequel to *Raiders*. That was the whole point of Spielberg and Lucas's initial reason for recreating the action-adventure serials of the past. 'I never considered it a sequel,' said Spielberg, 'it's a further adventure, another tale.' In fact, *Temple of Doom* was conceived more as a 'prequel' to *Raiders*, being set a year earlier than Indy's recovery of the lost Ark of the Covenant. But in juggling time, they were expecting to develop Indy's character more for, as Spielberg explained, our hero 'is not just a gravedigger, as in *Raiders*, obsessed with the material object of his quest. In this one he saves lives. Many lives. Young lives.' Little did they know that, in capitalizing upon the first film's success and the entry of Indiana Jones into folk lore, they were embarking upon a project the violence of which was to affect the entire structure by which 'young lives' were allowed access to such films. One scene caused particular controversy. In it a man has his heart plucked out by a priest as a human sacrifice. It was cut from the British cinema release. Spielberg defended the scene:

> The picture is not called the 'Temple of Roses' it is called the 'Temple of Doom'. I can remember as a child at the movies my parents used to cover my eyes in the cinema when they felt I should not be exposed to what was coming out of the screen: it was usually two people kissing innocently. There are parts of this film that are too intense for younger children but this is a fantasy adventure. It is the kind of violence that does not really happen, will not really happen and cannot really be perpetuated by people leaving the cinema and performing these tricks on their friends at home.

In late 1984, following the introduction of the new PG-13 (parental guidance) certificate that had been prompted by the popularity of *Temple of Doom* amongst American youngsters, Spielberg admitted that he would not like to see a 10-year-old admitted to the film and that 'the responsibility to the children of this country is worth any loss at the box office'.

For the sequel, Lucas recruited screenwriters Willard Huyck and Gloria Katz, with whom he had worked on *American Graffiti*. Having refused to make sequels for both *Jaws* and *CE3K*, Spielberg admitted that he had 'separation pangs' for both Lucas and the cast. 'I knew if I didn't

Harrison Ford as Indy in *Indiana Jones and the Temple of Doom*, 1984, the sequel to *Raiders of the Lost Ark*.

direct, somebody else would. I got a little bit jealous, I got a little bit frustrated and I signed on for one more'. He recognized, however, that

> The danger in making a sequel is that you can never satisfy everyone. If you give people the same movie with different scenes, they say 'Why weren't you more original?' But if you give them the same character in another fantastic adventure, but with a different *tone*, you risk disappointing the other half of the audience who just wanted a carbon copy of the first film with a different girl and a different bad guy. So you win and you lose both ways.

Filming began in the spring of 1983 with Spielberg predicting that 'it is going to have the same velocity as the first movie, and the humour and tempo are the same.' He underestimated himself.

The film begins with several famous tributes, the first to Paramount's mountain logo embossed on a large brass oriental gong in homage to *Gunga Din* (1939). The second tribute is to the great Busby Berkeley musicals of the past as Indy teams up in Shanghai with nightclub singer Willie Scott (Kate Capshaw) ominously singing Cole Porter's 'Anything

Goes' (in Chinese!). This beautifully choreographed scene, extending his earlier experiment in *1941*, demonstrates that Spielberg could indeed direct a musical as he one day intends to do (he has toyed with making a musical film of *Phantom of the Opera* for some time but he wants to ensure that the project is a huge spectacle: 'God knows I've been accused of enough of those, and I might as well add a musical to my crimes.') 'The result,' said *Newsweek's* reviewer, 'is an epic mêlée that seems choreographed by some crazy mutation of Mack Sennett and Twyla Tharp.'

In this film Spielberg showed the humorous touch that had eluded him for most of *1941*. It is the same sort of humour that made them name the lead characters after their dogs; Lucas's was called Indiana; Spielberg's Willie and Short Round was the name of the writers Huyck and Katz's dog.

Fearful that he would bore his audiences with this, his first sequel, Spielberg had put together a movie of such breathtaking pace that reviewer Jack Kroll commented: 'this movie has such unrelenting action that it jackhammers you into a punch-drunk stupor'. But what seemed to upset most reviewers was what they saw as excessive violence, one even describing the film as 'an astonishing violation of the trust people have in Spielberg and Lucas's essentially good-natured approach to movies intended primarily for kids'. Spielberg's response was that

> George . . . felt that he wanted this second Indiana Jones movie to contain moments of black magic, truly evil villains. You could say that the villains in the last film were evil, but they dealt in simple force. In this movie, our villains deal in black magic, torture and slavery. So they're *real* bad.

But Spielberg, in recreating the spirit of Imperial adventures of the past, was also accused of perpetuating the racism inherent in those films (although this was nothing compared to the charges made the following year when *The Color Purple* was released), not to mention their sexism. He clearly saw the Thuggies as comic book villains rather than anything else, admitting later that 'there's not an ounce of my personal feeling in *Temple of Doom*'. And although the film soon entered the top ten of all-time box office hits, grossing over $100 million, Spielberg later admitted that '*Indy Two* will not go down in my pantheon as one of my prouder moments.'

Indiana Jones and the Last Crusade (1989)

So why, five years later, did he decide to do a third Indiana Jones film? Spielberg explained:

> I'm no longer motivated much by money. I could make a whole bunch of

Harrison Ford as Indy with Sean Connery playing his father in *Indiana Jones and the Last Crusade*, 1989, which critics considered the best of the three Indiana Jones films.

pitiful movies, and I'd still be bankable for a while. That's Hollywood: people get something in their heads about you and that locks itself in . . . I'll give you a very good reason for doing *Indy 3*. When George first told me the story of *Raiders*, he said if it's a hit, will you give me a handshake promise to do two more? On that beach in Hawaii in 1979, we made a gentleman's agreement. We've remained friends and it's important to me not to let anything come between us. Also, those films are a lot of fun to do. Everything is just for the enjoyment of the public, what they want – what we think they want.

The opportunity could not have come at a better time. Just as *Raiders* helped to restore Spielberg's popular appeal after *1941*, *Indiana Jones and the Last Crusade* did the same thing following *Empire of the Sun* and the cancellation of his *Amazing Stories* on network television. He also wanted to make up for his personal disappointment with *Temple of*

Doom; this time 'I wanted to make a movie I could stand naked on top of.' Not that Paramount Studios any longer doubted the winning Lucasberger formula once American cinema chains started paying an unprecedented $40 million in unrefundable guarantees just for the rights to screen the film.

Spielberg's problem was in finding a formula that would appeal and provide a new challenge. Lucas and scriptwriter Jeffrey Boam found it for him: why not introduce Indy's dad? Spielberg was entranced with the notion, not least because of its time-juggling potential and its treatment of a father-son emotional reckoning, issues which were of personal concern to the director, who had now turned 40. His treatment of Indy's relationship with his father would come from the heart, from his own experience with Arnold. Besides, Spielberg, Lucas and Harrison Ford had all become fathers themselves recently. And as for casting Dr Henry Jones, Spielberg said, 'I thought, well, there's only one person in the entire universe who can play Indy's father, and that's Sean [Connery]'. Who better than the original James Bond to have given birth to this archaeologist adventurer and rogue?' Connery, Oscar winner for his supporting role in *The Untouchables*, agreed. Spielberg clearly enjoyed filming Ford and Connery together. 'The biggest thrill was putting Harrison and Sean in a two-shot and calling 'Action!' and trying not to ruin the take by laughing.' A $36 million budget was approved, locations in Spain, Venice, Jordan, London, Colorado, Utah and New Mexico identified, and filming began in May 1988.

Speaking about the second film, Spielberg explained what could be said for all three when he asked

> Is this Indiana Jones adventure worth the amount of emotional energy the audience has to give to the film? It's a group experience for large numbers of people sitting in movie theatres, not for two or three people sitting in front of the television at home. You need to feel the audience clapping and laughing and yelling and screaming in order to get the total effect of the Indiana Jones saga.

Considered by many to be the best of the three, *Last Crusade* captures all the action of *Raiders* and combines it with the emotional dimensions missing from *Temple of Doom*. The final scene, with Indiana riding into the sunset, is a combination of triumph and sadness and fully reflects Spielberg's own bittersweet feelings about completing a ten-year project with Lucas and the crew. 'It feels like the end of an era, and the end of a quest,' he said. If there are to be any more adventures, Spielberg said at the time, they would probably be without him as he planned to move on to quite different things.

THE COLOR PURPLE (1985)

He had in fact already ventured out into a different kind of project. Although it proved highly successful commercially, Spielberg's disappointment with *Temple of Doom* largely derived from the fact that he had not personally found the film particularly challenging. If not for his commitment to George Lucas to do a trilogy, he might well have sought a fresh challenge. He was conscious that he had done so much so quickly and that it was time for him to take stock and decide what he wanted to do next if he was to sustain his interest with a craft he had mastered so early. His decision to make his next film, untypically about people who are not larger than the story, both excited and terrified him. 'It's the risk of being judged,' he said, 'and accused of not having the sensibility to do character studies.' He was about to enter his busiest production period and to return to television anthologies with his *Amazing Stories* series for NBC. But, as a director, he needed a personal challenge. 'It's as if I've been swimming in water up to my waist all my life and I'm great at it – but now I'm going into the deep section of the pool.'

Spielberg's decision to make *The Color Purple* was prompted by Kathleen Kennedy who gave him a copy of Alice Walker's book, not as a potential project for him to film, but merely to read. He explained:

> She gave me some background: 'You know it's a black story. But that shouldn't bother you, because you're Jewish and essentially you share similarities in your upbringing and your heritage.' I had some anti-Semitic experiences when I was growing up that Kathleen knew about, including prejudice and everything else that I had to go through at one particular high school. So I read the book and I loved it, but I didn't want to direct it. Then I picked it up again about a month and a half later, and I read it a second time. And I couldn't get away from certain images.

He knew it would be a departure for him, and he retained his reservations about his suitability to direct. When he asked the co-producer, Quincy Jones, 'Don't you want to find a black director, or a woman?', he was met with the answer: 'You didn't have to come from Mars to do *E.T.*, did you?' What really attracted him, he said elsewhere, 'was the chance to make a movie that relied on characters to tell a story, not a story to reveal the characters.' He had tried 'unsuccessfully' in *1941* to 'do a movie where I could juggle eleven characters' and he became keen to 'redeem himself'.

Both films have ensemble casts, and I've only worked in two or three or four – character pieces. The danger is that you get lost in the flood of new characters who come in and out of the movie. But I think that in America it is a lot easier. It may sound crass and callous to say this, but we're so used to watching soap opera television – *Dynasty*, *The Colbys*, *Dallas*, *Knott's Landing*, and the day-time soap operettas, that the American appetite for being able to collate and separate one character from one another is better than it was 15 or 20 years ago.

Apart from the fact that the film's overseas success would also be helped by the same phenomenon, which is part of the Americanization of world culture, he knew that if he made the film he would have to avoid the temptation to use America's most celebrated black stars, such as Diana Ross (who one can envisage in the role of Shug Avery), not least because their audience appeal might detract from the story itself.

Having been reduced to tears by the novel, which is written in the form of letters between two sisters over 40 years, Quincy Jones introduced him to Alice Walker at her San Francisco home and, over dinner, they discussed his vision of her book. 'She has a kind of beneficence about her, a light,' he said of Walker. 'She's very kind, which I respond to. We talked for hours, and we really hit it off.' Spielberg was undoubtedly attracted by the author's portrayal of broken families, the impact of separation, the sensitive treatment of women and children and the elements of loneliness, innocence, endurance and survival in the character of Celie – all issues that had permeated his previous films. 'It links to my previous movies in that it portrays an urgency to fulfil a dream,' he said. They agreed, for example, on such matters as casting. Miss Walker suggested Whoopi Goldberg, an up-and-coming comedienne then playing nightclubs in San Francisco, who had written to her praising her book, for the part of Celie. Spielberg asked her to audition at Amblin Entertainment's custom-built theatre, in front of such close friends as Michael Jackson, Quincy Jones and Lionel Ritchie: 'she blew us all away. She turned out to be a wonderful, wonderful actress'. However, being inexperienced as an actress, Goldberg found herself intimidated during rehearsals by the 'professionalism' of Danny Glover and the 'spontaneity' of Oprah Winfrey. Spielberg was worried that she would not fit in until she said to him: 'Listen, you're going to have to help me because I don't know what the hell I'm doing.'

Spielberg said of her Oscar-nomination performance: 'That performance came out of her soul.' But Goldberg was happy to pay tribute to Spielberg's direction of her and the film laid to rest the charge that Spielberg was better working with special effects and children than with mature actors. It also laid to rest Walker's initial concerns about

Spielberg directing Celie (Whoopi Goldberg) in *The Color Purple*, 1985. Spielberg called this film 'my people picture . . . not a black movie – but a movie about people everywhere'. Some critics, however, were deeply offended by his 'Spielbergization' of Alice Walker's highly acclaimed novel – but not Walker herself.

entrusting her book to a white director. 'My colour was never an issue after she selected me as the right guy for the picture. The issue was not the colour of my skin, but whether I'd make a good movie out of the book.' Walker was on the set for about half of the time, advising constantly on issues of production design and ensuring that Spielberg's changes were in keeping with the spirit of her novel. One of the major changes Spielberg made was to cut the lesbian relationship between Celie and Shug that features in the novel. He leaves this to the imagination of his audience and was inevitably criticized for doing so. But as he explained,

> The power of the cinema is a lot stronger than the power of literature, because more people have access to it for one thing, and a picture is worth a thousand words. The kiss on the lips to me in *The Color Purple* is so suggestive of the bringing together of those two characters in a sexual way, I just didn't feel I had to beat the audience over the head by showing

anything beyond that bonding. Anything more and the emphasis of the film would have shifted – there would have been just too much on that one taboo.

For her part, Walker seems to have been impressed with Spielberg's direction of the performances, of which he has said:

> It's important not to stage the shot in your head when you're working with actors, especially with a movie like *The Color Purple*. I blocked it like you would a play – you want to give the actors a chance to feel natural as they move about. Then I step back and take some time to figure out how I want to co-ordinate the scene. Not just the master shot, but where the coverage will be. It takes time, with the crew wondering, 'Doesn't he know what he's doing? He's not giving us a shot. He's just pacing back and forth.'

Spielberg drew upon all his own memories of separation for the painful scene in which the two sisters are driven apart by Mister. It is a powerful portrayal of loss as the two sisters play pattycake from a distance. Alice Walker was on the set when the scene was filmed. Spielberg said:

> I did the master in one shot because I wanted everyone to experience what the separation was like. I didn't want to have to say, 'OK, go down the steps of the porch. Cut. Have lunch.' I wanted the actors to feel the horror. And you can't do that when you piecemeal a scene. So I did it in one shot, and I turned to Alice and she was a wreck. Really crying. And that was good for me because I wanted to impress her. This was her book; she'd won the Pulitzer Prize.

So Spielberg assembled as many principal crewmen that he knew he could work with as possible, especially Allen Daviau, who had filmed *Amblin* (one of Spielberg's early short films as director) and, more recently, *E.T.* for him, as director of photography, and Michael Kahn, who had worked with him on four of his previous five films, as editor. So keen had he become to make the film that he agreed to take only the Directors Guild of America minimum salary of $40,000, much of which he poured back when the film began to strain its $15 million budget.

Set in America's deep south during the first third of the twentieth century, *The Color Purple* is the story of Celie (Whoopi Goldberg), a black girl subjected to mental and physical cruelty when she is 'given' by her incestuous father to a widower, Albert (Danny Glover), whom she calls 'Mister'. Although slavery had long been renounced, the story traces Celie's 40-year struggle to renounce its effective perpetuation by bigoted men. She is forced to look after Mister's house and family and respond to his brutal advances. The only way she can sustain herself amidst this

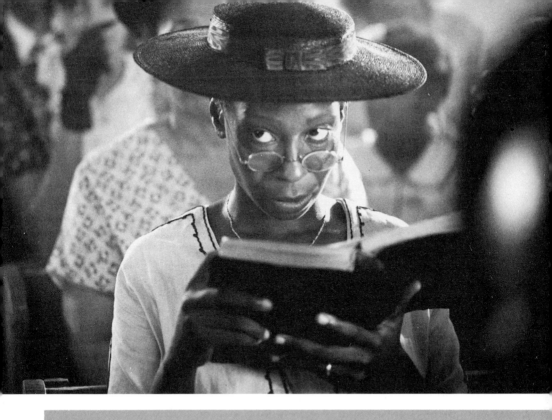

Celie in *The Color Purple*, 1985. Whoopie Goldberg's performance earned one of the film's 11 Oscar nominations – but not one for its director.

misery is through her letters from her sister, Nettie (Akosua Busia), who has been forcefully separated from Celie by Mister and who has gone to Africa as a missionary. Because he cannot penetrate this aspect of Celie's life in order to dominate it, Mister intercepts the letters and hides them from Celie. Although she is almost broken as a result, Celie is lifted by the arrival of Shug Avery (Margaret Avery), a glamorous blues singer who is Mister's lover but who also provides Celie with inspiration, courage and hope until her sister's return.

Having recognized from the outset that this film was a departure for him and that he had a considerable responsibility to the novel and to Alice Walker, Spielberg announced that he was 'for the first time almost satisfied, *almost*, with the way a film turned out. Now it's time away.' But the by now growing band of Spielberg detractors were just waiting for a chance to have a go at the 'Spielbergization' of Walker's highly respected novel. While he personally concentrated on spending time with his newly born son Max (amazingly, Amy Irving went into labour during the filming of Celie's childbirth), the knives came out. His African sequences were unfairly compared with Sydney Pollack's *Out of Africa*, which was released at about the same time and was to prove the film's main Oscar rival (winning seven to *Purple's* none). Spielberg did in fact underplay these scenes deliberately to enable the story in the film to be kept centrally in Celie's imagination, rather than shift to Nettie's real experiences of Africa that forms half of the novel. His decision to concentrate on Celie's innocence rather than upon Nettie's more educated and wider perspective of events enables Spielberg to highlight the parallel of white oppression of blacks with male oppression of women.

> Some people wanted the movie to be about the tumbledown, ramshackle Deep South. But Alice Walker's grandparents were well off, they were successful, and we based Celie and Mister's house on pictures Alice showed us. We took criticism . . . for the art direction from people who weren't aware that her grandparents were wealthy by the standards of the day. I think some people had a kind of *Uncle Tom's Cabin* view of what the picture should be, which is wrong. And, ironically, it pointed out their own inclination for racial stereotyping, which is what some of the same people said we were guilty of.

Spielberg was particularly puzzled by a backlash from certain sections of the black community in America, which accused him of depicting black males as cruel sexists. 'I never saw the movie in any way as reinforcing those stereotypes', he said. 'This is a human story, and the film is about human beings. It's about men and women. This is a movie about the triumph of the spirit – and spirit and soul never had any racial boundaries.' Whoopi Goldberg said in an interview:

> Sometimes black men in the movie abuse black women. Now people see lots of movies where white men abuse white women, and they never think 'This movie stereotypes whites.' Steven has made a fantastic movie about the human experience. There is not a 'mammy' or a 'nigger' in this film. I resent the fact that people think we actors would be involved in something that shows stereotyped behaviour. Do people think that neither I am capable of judging what's exploitative, nor Danny Glover nor Oprah Winfrey?

He took comfort from Alice Walker's satisfaction with the final result: 'She's seen the movie now many times. We were hoping for her blessings, and she was overly generous.' Yet the attacks on Spielberg and the film continued, particularly on American television, where Spielberg was accused of over-sentimentalizing Celie's plight, minimizing Nettie's role and of either playing up or playing down the racial and feminist issues of the novel.

The knives may have been out, but the people went to the box office.

Despite this, and despite his track record on films dealing with different subjects, the man who cried at the novel was surprised at the film's popular success:

> I thought *The Color Purple* had a very low concept. I didn't think anybody would go to see that movie, which made over $100,000,000 in America. And I thought that was my art film. I thought, 'My God, it's got an all black cast and all-black films have never really been that successful, except a couple of police pictures,' and so that surprised me.

What also surprised him was the furore that erupted when the film was nominated for 11 Academy Awards but not one for its director. And when the film failed to win a single Oscar, he could only reflect silently upon the criticisms that had been levelled against him that were now being directed against the Motion Picture Academy for being racist for ignoring the film.

EMPIRE OF THE SUN (1987)

After *The Color Purple* and the birth of his son, Spielberg took – by his standards – a prolonged period away from directing movies, although he did direct two episodes of his new *Amazing Stories* television series ('The Mission' and 'Ghost Train') and was still working as executive producer on such films as *Back to the Future*, *The Money Pit*, *The Goonies*, *Young Sherlock Holmes*, *An American Tail* and *Innerspace*. The workaholic could not really stop. On *The Goonies*, for example, 'a film I didn't want to direct but I did want to see', the director Richard Donner (of *Superman* fame) testified to Spielberg's constant presence on the set: 'he was over my shoulder the whole time. But he has so many good ideas you just want to grab them.' Spielberg was in many respects awaiting a film script that could rekindle his passion; he had had to write *Close Encounters* himself and he had had so much personal input into the writing of *E.T.*, but he harboured no more 'dream projects' for the moment, now that the birth of Max had prompted him (temporarily) to abandon his long-standing desire to film *Peter Pan*. He became frustrated at the failure of other people's scriptwriting to really fire him up. This was one reason why he made that speech saying it was 'time to renew our romance with the word' when receiving the Thalberg Award in 1986. Having been satisfied with his incursion into more dialogue-oriented films with *The Color Purple*, he decided he would have to again turn to a novel if he was to continue his process of branching out from his established style. This time he turned to British writing, J.G. Ballard's

Spielberg with Christian Bale who plays Jamie in *Empire of the Sun*, 1987, his most 'British' film to date.

1984 book *Empire of the Sun*, and to write the screenplay he employed British playwright Tom Stoppard (of *Rosencrantz and Guildenstern are Dead* fame).

Stoppard had initially been commissioned to write a script by producer Robert Shapiro of Warner Brothers but, when Spielberg showed interest, Kathleen Kennedy and Frank Marshall worked out a deal that Amblin would do the film for the studio. It was to be Spielberg's most British movie to date, with a British scriptwriter converting an Englishman's book into a film that had a largely British cast. A nice little irony is that David Lean had at one time shown interest in making the film. When Ballard first met Spielberg, once filming of various interior sequences had begun in London, the director asked him to play a non-speaking part as a guest dressed as John Bull at the fancy dress party near the start of the film. Although cut from the final film, the writer's impressions were highly favourable:

> But it was very generous of him and I was profoundly impressed by him. I
> liked him enormously, and in fact within five seconds of talking to him, I

knew that my book was in the best possible hands. He struck me as a man with a very powerful, hard imagination – completely *unsentimental*, quite the opposite of what I had read in the newspapers; he was completely dedicated to tackling the book in the most serious possible way.

Ballard deliberately kept his contribution to a minimum, recording a voice-over introduction for the start of the film, because he did not want the technical exercise of filmmaking to detract from his own enjoyment of the finished film: 'I want to be able to sit back in the audience like everybody else and be captivated by the magic of Steven Spielberg.'

The film of Ballard's semi-autobiographical novel about his childhood in wartime Shanghai is a difficult one to describe in terms of its content, largely because of its reliance upon the visual performance of the film's principal character, Jim Graham (the J. G. of Ballard), played by Christian Bale in his first screen role. This might seem surprising until one considers Stoppard's script, a relatively busy one in terms of dialogue but one which simplifies and adapts the novel for visual purposes. The collaboration worked so well that not only did they become great friends but Spielberg also contracted Stoppard to work for Amblin reading books and screenplays. Spielberg said in 1990:

> It's a good partnership because what I think I've done is to introduce Tom to telling the story with pictures and Tom introduced me to telling the story with dialogue. He showed me an interesting way of talking, not to the point but round the point. You don't just come out and say what you mean. Let the audience figure it out for themselves. Give them all the clues and then confirm, after they figure it out, that they were right.

As a result, although all the usual spectacular visual imagery is still very much in evidence, as are the aeroplanes, the themes of childhood, separation, survival, surrogate parenthood and so on, *Empire of the Sun* also tackles the *death* of innocence and, as such, is perhaps Spielberg's most complex film to date.

Critics greeted the film with a recognition that Spielberg was attempting to mature on screen. They saw Jim's character as an analogy for Spielberg himself, the boy who was forced to grow up because of the unpleasant world in which he found himself. As Richard Corliss wrote:

> In war, even in this Spielberg war, wisdom brings bitter lessons. It teaches Jim that he may – must – filch food from the dying and take shoes from the dead. When P-51s zoom above him, the plane-crazy boy crash-dives into delirium; his dreams have singed him by flying too close, poisoned him with their oil and cordite . . . No child can see all this and hold onto childhood.

Jamie's American-inspired attempt to get outside the wire of the prison-camp in *Empire of the Sun*, 1987. Once again, Spielberg demonstrated his remarkable capacity to extract extraordinary performances from child actors.

Derek Malcolm claimed that the film's chief lesson was that 'children have the capacity to swim against the tide even more strongly than adults, because they fabricate their own world, whatever the circumstances'. Despite the horrors to which he was subjected, Spielberg refuses to admit the triumph of evil as Jim is eventually reunited with his real parents. Spielberg's conclusion ran as follows:

> I thought *Empire of the Sun* was a 'high concept'. When that film didn't perform, I was a bit surprised. Not that I'd got so used to success but just simply because I thought *Empire of the Sun* wasn't a journey into misery – it was about the death of innocence – but it turned off a lot of people in America. A lot of audiences said 'well, this isn't typecasting for him so I don't think I'm going to give this film a chance' because it seems like a film that, if John Boorman's name was on it or even someone else's, they might give it a chance.

The film was inevitably compared with Boorman's *Hope and Glory*, which came out at about the same time and which received much more recognition. In Britain, controversy erupted when the film was selected for the Royal Film Performance in March 1988. Survivors of the Japanese occupation resented the film's portrayal of the British community although they resented more Ballard's child's eye view than Spielberg's. The director pointed out that 'it was Ballard who saw them as raucous and filled with spite and vinegar, and the British dormitory as a more lethargic type of place'. He was right to point out that the image conflicted sharply with the stiff-upper-lip, British bulldog Blitz survivor view held by most Americans – which was one reason why the Anglophile Spielberg was so interested in Ballard's book in the first place. He added: 'John Boorman's film is much more positive: the memories are extremely non-toxic, the boy is going to grow up and lead a normal life.'

In America, critics liked the film's complexity and profundity, although Pauline Kael remained uncertain as to what it was actually about. But the overall reaction of critics and audiences alike was disappointment at Spielberg's sombre tone. Spielberg's reply was to say:

> I got a bollocking from critics who didn't like the idea that I was suddenly trying to stretch my character. There are certain people in America who want to keep me young; that makes them feel safe. But I've had ten years, and a lot of success, in a certain genre of movie. Now I have to explore other forms, to shake myself out of what every artist fears, which is lethargy and apathy. I'm looking forward to a new and unusual ten years.

ALWAYS (1989)

Although *Always* is set in the present day, it has all the feel of a film from the great days of Hollywood, being a remake (or 'reworking', as Spielberg prefers to call it) of the 1943 Spencer Tracy – Irene Dunne vehicle, *A Guy Named Joe*. It was a film he had wanted to make for well over ten years but it took him some time to feel sufficiently confident to make a romantic comedy involving an adult love affair. He had first seen the original Victor Fleming film on television when he was 14: 'it was the second movie that ever made me cry that didn't have a deer in it. And it's a reassuring story. It's about life and saying it while you're here and doing it while you can.' Once again, then, Spielberg was returning to his own memories and experiences to motivate his filmmaking, and although it is his first film since *Duel* not to feature children in a central role (interestingly, the only time children appear in both films is on a school bus, but then only to highlight the adult plight), it does tackle issues that reverberate through-out all of Spielberg's films: separation, loneliness, a recognition and acceptance of fate and destiny, a resigned renunciation of partnerships, the mysteries of flight. All these had been evident in *Empire of the Sun* and even the third Indiana Jones film, but had been largely subsumed by the action. Here was his chance to consolidate his efforts at character studies launched properly with *The Color Purple*.

He had in fact discussed the idea of making the film during the making of *Jaws* with Richard Dreyfuss, a great Tracy fan who had seen the 1943 version 'a serious 30 or 40 times', and again with him during the filming of *Close Encounters*. 'If you cast anybody else in the part of Pete [the part played by Tracy] I'll kill you,' Dreyfuss told the director. A screenplay was in fact commissioned in 1980, with Spielberg envisaging Robert Redford and Paul Newman in the leading male roles. 'They both quite liked the notion of the story, but both of them wanted to play Pete . . . and so I couldn't make that work.' Besides, 'I couldn't find my leading lady.' But the main factor that stopped him, he admitted, was that 'I wasn't mature enough emotionally then.' As the 1980s unfolded, this began to change but, even though he conceded to Dreyfuss's 'threat' and found John Goodman for the part of Al (Ward Bond in the original) after seeing him play opposite Roseanne Barr in the hit TV comedy *Roseanne*,

Spielberg directing *Always*, 1989.

the role of Dorinda remained a problem. Then he went to see William Hurt and Holly Hunter in *Broadcast News* in 1988, and he was so impressed by her performance that '10 or 15 minutes in I said to myself: 'I've got my cast, isn't it wonderful, I've got my cast.'

The problem was he hadn't yet got his script. Having worked successfully with Tom Stoppard on *Empire of the Sun*, he asked the British playwright to draft out several versions. Stoppard did so, though the final credit goes to Jerry Belson. Spielberg remained undecided 'about the movie's tone; where the story should go; what kind of departure I wanted to make from the original'. By 1988, he had decided that although 'this is the only remake I would ever consider directing myself', he would bring the old story of a Second World War pilot who is killed and returns to earth as an invisible but influential presence up to date by turning the leading protagonists into firefighters.

Steven Spielberg's proven filmic love affair with aeroplanes is brilliantly confirmed in the opening shot of the movie. In this sequence, we see a Catalina flying boat almost colliding with two fishermen on a lake. Spielberg's much beloved aircraft serve to fix our thoughts firmly in the past, as is the use of engine-driven aircraft by the leading characters Pete Sandich (Richard Dreyfuss) and Al (John Goodman), aerial forest firefighters with their planes painted 'Fire-eaters'. Helicopters, dialogue and the emancipated Dorinda played by Holly Hunter, quickly tell us that it is a contemporary setting. But the feel is pure 1940s. Spielberg said of Hunter that she was 'Everygirl – feisty, smart and extremely opinionated'. He admitted that 'I've always been attracted to forthright women who aren't afraid to lay it on the line, even if sometimes that line goes right across our chests.'

Spielberg confessed that *Always* was not a hard film to make, especially compared to *Last Crusade*, which was on a much larger scale. This was a very intimate film, a true labour of love. Once again, one of his films was chosen to be premiered before the Royal Family. At least this time the Queen didn't have to sit through it with her fingers in her ears for most of the time, as she reportedly did with *Close Encounters*. But the critical reaction to *Always* was surprisingly muted. It wasn't a blockbuster, like *Last Crusade* or the *Back to the Future* sequels or even like *Gremlins II*, all of which did far better business for Amblin in the 12-month period surrounding *Always'* release. Perhaps, as a 'small' film, the remake merely got lost amidst the more effectively-hyped sequels. But Spielberg had confessed that the original version was 'the film that taught me how to make love to women' and in many ways we can see a great deal of how Spielberg sees himself in the character of Pete, as well as Dreyfuss's self-image – which is why they are such good friends. Many critics found

Pete (Richard Dreyfuss) is the unseen, unheard presence who sees the woman he loves, Dorinda (Holly Hunter) in the arms of Ted (Brad Johnson) the pilot he is sent back to Earth to inspire, in *Always*, 1989.

the film childish in its portrayal of an adult love affair, with Pete/ Dreyfuss/Spielberg ultimately being saved from having to tackle responsibly for a serious relationship by death. They would have preferred to have kept the original setting because at least under wartime conditions such inflated romanticism was more acceptable, more comprehensible, than in a more contemporary context. For this reason, the first half of the film, while Pete is still alive, works better than the second, when he is dead, although the best human scene in the film does come when Pete, unseen, dances with Dorinda to the tune of 'Smoke Gets In Your Eyes'. It is, in fact, a highly charming film, appealing to fans of the old Hollywood romantic comedies of Tracy and Hepburn and of such wonderful period pieces as *The Fighting Sullivans* (1944). Spielberg had (following *The Color Purple*) made another film that was less obviously 'a Steven Spielberg film' than anything he had done since *Sugarland Express*. In many ways, it represented the sort of films he would like to have been turning out regularly if he had been born a few decades earlier and been able to work in the golden age of Hollywood.

4

Spielberg and the American Future

I've never given up the ghost of my childhood. I've been hanging on to that. I really feel I stopped developing emotionally when I was 19. I really believe we're all children! . . . Because I'm an adult now, I can really ride the fence, ride herd on both feelings.

Whatever else Spielberg may be, he is an unashamed sentimentalist, an optimistic romantic who looks forward to a better world in which people learn to confront and overcome their fears – just as he himself has tried to do all his own life. He uses film rather like a psychiatrist tackling a phobia – not just for his patients, the audience, but for himself. We have seen how in *Jaws* he brilliantly exploited the fear of what lies beneath the water's surface and how in *Duel* he manipulated fears of faceless drivers who sit behind the wheel of those gigantic trucks that creep up in our rear-view mirrors. In both cases, the potential victim has reluctantly to confront a widely held fear on behalf of all of us who have ever swam in the ocean or driven on the highway, and to overcome it – often at great personal risk. Even in the escapist Indiana Jones films, our hero has to overcome his childhood fear of snakes. But the message throughout his films is that the victim can triumph against the odds through courage and ingenuity (or, in the case of *1941*, by accident) – and hope. That message is in the finest Hollywood tradition.

Yet in one area, Spielberg has broken with an established genre of Hollywood film-making in a significant departure for which he deserves recognition. He is really the first American film-maker to tackle the possibility that alien life might actually be friendly rather than hostile. His two major contributions to this mould-breaking portrayal, *Close Encounters of the Third Kind* and *E.T. – The Extra Terrestrial*, were important contributions to the notion that human beings need not necessarily fear creatures from outer space.

The idea that 'We Are Not Alone' (the marketing slogan on posters for *Close Encounters*) was not, of course, new to Hollywood films. But virtually all previous science fiction films did not merely ignore the possibility that alien life could be friendly, they actually cultivated a fear that, if it did exist out there, it was bound to be hostile – or at least want something that it was prepared to take by force. Even the apparently benign and ostensibly humanoid Klaatu (played by Michael Rennie) in *The Day the Earth Stood Still* (1951) brings with him a robot, in the form of Gort, with destructive powers to enforce his message that man must abandon his course of self-annihilation through the development of nuclear weapons or else have that decision made for him by beings who know better. In films where aliens didn't actually look like humans, the case was even more clear-cut: they were downright hostile, and their ugliness reinforced the point.

After generations of indoctrination along this particular line of thinking, once again Spielberg tackled our fears head-on and came up with an optimistic solution that pushed a range of emotional buttons that made us weep with wonder and hope. Despite always being an avid comic-book reader and science fiction film-goer:

> I always felt that space creatures were given an unfair shake by Hollywood. Aliens would come to Earth, land, look around and kill everything in sight. Or, we shoot first, they shoot back and then, of course, mad scientists, Earth scientists, go into a room, invent a contraption in four days and shoot all the flying saucers down.

As Spielberg recognized, science fiction films had always been a very real extension of twentieth century earthly fears concerning war and invasion. As a reflective mirror on society, the medium of cinema could scarcely neglect the historic times that formed the backdrop against which it was flourishing – world wars, genocide and the development of technology capable of devastating the entire planet. The portrayal of aliens as technologically advanced creatures capable of reaching Earth inevitably resulted in accrediting aliens with Earth-like human qualities and motives drawn from the planet's history – aggression, colonization and invasion. These were the very stuff of such films as *Invaders from Mars* (1951, remade by Tobe Hooper in 1986), *Invasion of the Body Snatchers* (1953, remade by Philip Kaufman in 1978) and *Invasion of the Saucer Men* (1957). 'Comics and TV always portrayed aliens as malevolent,' said Spielberg. 'I *never* believed that. If they had the technology to get here, they could only be benign.'

In George Pal's 1953 adaptation of H.G. Wells' classic novel *War of the Worlds*, the Earth's invaders are seen as colonizers and indiscriminate killers of human life, not defeated by Earth's technology (including nuclear weapons) but by a micro-organism so small and so harmless to humanity that it had almost been forgotten about. The final sequence, in which the Martian spaceships collapse outside a church full of worshippers whose only hope is God, hints at a highly spiritual salvation in which the aliens are clearly godless and, ultimately, stupid for not recognizing the fatal nature of the tiny virus. A tantalizing note is struck by the outstretched arm of a dying alien that emerges from the collapsed spaceship, implying a creature so horrible that we are not allowed to see its whole form.

In *Close Encounters*, Spielberg broke the mould by actually showing us the entire creature – with elongated limbs reminiscent of that final scene in *War of the Worlds* – but with a smiling face. Again, in *E.T.* we see the alien's face and although it is admittedly ugly, it is a lovable, big-eyed but small-framed extra terrestrial who is as much afraid of human beings as they are of it. This simple suggestion, that they just might be as afraid of us as we are of them despite their superior technology, is a device used by Spielberg to disarm generations of fear perpetuated by Hollywood's science fiction films from the Cold War era.

Prior to *CE3K* and *E.T.*, aliens had either been colossal bug-eyed monsters or creatures that took the shape, form and appearance of humans. The bug-eyed variety were easy to identify as evil threats; but the humanoid versions were more sinister. They represented the fear of their time – a fear of an enemy within, subversives who looked and behaved much like us but who were really plotting the downfall of civilization as we know it. They were a 'fifth column', distinguished perhaps only by a high forehead or shocking white hair, but essentially the evil within us all. It is not hard to imagine how such films played on fears current in the 1940s and 1950s about Nazi 'fifth columnists' or 'red traitors'. They were alien beings from alien cultures with alien philosophies who were all the more dangerous because they looked like us, and were thus difficult to identify easily. The moral was: be on guard; the price of freedom is eternal vigilance. It fitted well with the atmosphere of the Cold War.

By the early 1980s, however, with the advent of Ronald Reagan and his programme to restore confidence to an American society gradually coming to terms with the defeat of Vietnam, Spielberg instinctively felt that

people want to believe in something. *E.T.* is a happily pacifistic film. I thought the spirit of youth, so to speak, is sort of in every person. Everybody can identify with their own childhood. To have an E.T. in your life just keeps you young all your life. I think you have to believe in something.

He had begun the process with *Close Encounters*, which has hints of menace before the realization that the visitors are benign. But with *E.T. – The Extra Terrestrial* we know right from the outset that Hollywood's traditional hunters have become the hunted.

E.T. is undoubtedly Spielberg's masterpiece. Made at a cost of a mere $10.3 million, with about 10 per cent of the budget going on the development of the creature itself, it remains the highest grossing movie of all time. Spielberg himself has described it as his most personal film to date, corresponding closest to his own innermost memories, experiences and fantasies:

> I can't really say that *E.T.* dropped out of the sky and hit me on the head without a number of experiences from the time my father made me go with him at 3am to watch a meteor shower when I was six years old and I suddenly realized that the sky up there and the stars are worthy of closer scrutiny – all the way to the time I saw *The Wizard of Oz* and *Peter Pan* and every Disney film ever made and all the films of Hitchcock and Kubrick and read all the novels of Steinbeck and Faulkner and all the experiences I ever had in elementary and grammar school and high school and college to bring me to a place in my life where I found myself standing in the Sahara Desert shooting *Raiders of the Lost Ark* . . . lonely and depressed, making this crazy movie with dust and airplanes and whips and snakes . . . and, indeed, something *did* fall out of the sky and hit me on the head in the shape of a small, fat, little, squashy character named E.T.

Spielberg was 34 years old when he started to make the film. In it, he demonstrated, or rather consolidated, a skill in directing children few film-makers have ever equalled to produce a family fantasy film that appeals to children of all ages. He remembered Truffaut's advice, given on the set of *Close Encounters*, about children being ideal actors because they were so keen to please without being hampered by ego and just wanted to have a good time. Spielberg now revelled in their spontaneity and instinctive desire to please.

Few of the millions who have seen *E.T.* will ever forget the experience of viewing it for the first time. Still fewer will recall an audience completely unmoved by it. Martin Amis described the audience reaction in Los Angeles:

> Towards the end of *E.T.*, barely able to support my own grief and

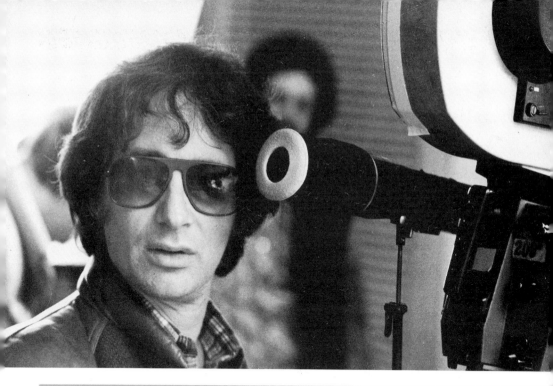

Spielberg directs *ET The Extra-Terrestrial*, 1982. Spielberg's undoubted masterpiece, and lowest budget film, eschews special effects in favour of the story, for which the director plunged deeply into his own experience and imagination.

bewilderment, I turned and looked down the aisle at my fellow sufferers: executive, black dude, Japanese businessman, punk, hippie, mother, teenage, child. Each face was a mask of tears. Staggering out, through a tundra of sodden hankies, I felt drained, pooped, squeezed dry; I felt I had lived out a one-year love affair – complete with desire and despair, passion and prostration – in the space of 120 minutes.

Even the most cynical were reduced to sniffles as a funny-looking alien with a neck capable of being elongated like a telescope strikes up a friendship with a small boy, Elliott (played by Henry Thomas), and as the alien-child partnership combine in an effort to enable the stranded visitor to return to his own world. We share the dilemma of whether the friendship struck up in the process can survive the ostensibly huge gap in cultures. We are united in supporting them as the film brilliantly overcomes any prejudices we might possess concerning the wisdom of a friendship or partnership between two such different types of being. We are similarly united in viewing Elliott's efforts on behalf of his alien friend as a noble cause deserving of our support despite the fact that he is combating our own kind – humans, or rather adults, with an inevitable curiosity about this alien visitor. We want E.T. to stay and be happy here but recognize that this can never be so while humans hunt him down in their quest for scientific knowledge. So we want E.T. to escape this curiosity in the belief that he will be happier with his own kind until a time in the future when we have learned to accept others different from ourselves for what they are. The price that we, the audience, have to pay is Elliott's (and Spielberg's), namely the separation of a friendship amidst the dilemma of one asking the other to 'stay' while the other asks him to come with him. The moral is that friendship between cultures is possible amongst the young and the innocent, but not quite yet feasible in a cynical, adult world which has forgotten the meaning of true friendship and understanding.

It is a wonderful movie, which appeals to audiences steeped in the cynicism of the post-war world but seduced by age-old Hollywood fantasies about the way the world really should be. 'I always considered it a love story, even before the script was written. That was going to be my love story.' *Time* magazine described it as 'a miracle movie, and one that confirms Spielberg as a master story-teller of his medium'. He had thought of filming a story he had written in 1979, entitled 'Night Skies' and had handed it over to screenwriter John Sayles who produced hostile aliens rather than the one Spielberg had in mind. Exactly what that was, Spielberg recalled, came during the filming of *Raiders* in Tunisia:

> I remember when I finally sat down and wrote the idea for *E.T.*, it was in the Sahara desert where I was working on *Raiders*. I was lonely with no one to talk to; my girlfriend was in California and so was George Lucas. Harrison Ford was ill and I wished I had a friend. Then I thought about being ten years old, which I've sort of been all my life, and about feeling like that. And I began inventing this little creature based on the guy who steps out of the mothership in *Close Encounters*.

He discussed the idea with Melissa Mathison, the co-writer of *The Black Stallion* (1979) who was in the desert as Harrison Ford's girlfriend at the time. She recalled that the writing of the screenplay was essentially a collaborative effort even though 'E.T. was already half-created in Steven's mind. He wanted him to be tender and to communicate emotionally rather than intellectually.' She continued:

> We did a lot of pitching back and forth of ideas. And everyone put in his two cents about the E.T. himself. I wanted him to be benevolent – E.T.s always seem to be hostile and violent. Steven wanted him to be emotional. I always wanted him to be shorter than the children so he was always little.

Then the neck came in. I have a little drawing in my notebook when I was telling Steven he looked like a turtle and we both sort of looked at each other and that's when the neck came in. When that neck goes up, you know it's not somebody in a suit.

Working on a plot originally called 'Growing Up' which became 'After School' and then 'A Boy's Life', Mathison drew heavily upon Spielberg's own childhood memories, especially since all Spielberg's instincts told him that 'now's the time to bring my little friend down from the stars'. He also felt it was time to exorcise his childhood nightmares – but *E.T.* was not the right place. That form of self-therapy was to be achieved with *Poltergeist* made around the same time. Mathison had begun writing in earnest as Spielberg was editing *Raiders* late in 1980 and found herself fuelled by the passion of Spielberg's recollections. Bored with making mega-films with huge budgets, and correspondingly huge studio expectations, he had long threatened to make 'something I really wanted to make . . . a movie involving young people'. Of the adults in the film Spielberg said:

> It was very important to me that adults not be part of this children's world – visibly, that they have no identity until it's crucial to the story. I remember the cartoons of Warner Brothers and MGM, of Chuck Jones, of Fritz Freleng, Tex Avery, of all the great cartoonists in the forties. Often they'd choose small characters – mainly cats and dogs. But you'd never see the adults. You'd only see their legs . . . You *never* saw the character! And I remembered that for an adult to violate a cartoon world was a terrible mistake. I drew a parallel with that.

After all, he had nothing to lose, nothing left to prove to anybody – except himself. The badness was to be channelled into *Poltergeist* and the goodness into *E.T.*, which he began by his usual story-boarding of the film. He soon decided to abandon his time-honoured technique for fear of blocking himself off from his emotional input as he began filming in September 1981. 'I decided, this once, to take a chance. Just came on to the set and winged it every day and made the movie as close to my own sensibilities and instincts as I possibly could.'

'The emotion of the last scene was genuine,' said Spielberg. 'The final days of shooting were the saddest I've experienced on a film set.' As he laid down the music score to this scene, Williams turned to Spielberg and said: 'It's shameless. Will we get away with it?' to which came the reply: 'Movies *are* shameless.'

The film was first shown at the Cannes Film Festival on 26 May 1982. Its critical acclaim there, followed by its massive success at the box-office, was deeply satisfying to Spielberg since it was his most personal film to date. The film is carried by the children (there are only two main adults in the plot and they are there purely to serve as counterpoints to the children's plight). But it is the central, simple dilemma faced by the children that is at the heart of the film's appeal. When E.T. is unwittingly stranded on Earth, not only is he a stranger in a strange, threatening land but also it is human (or, more particularly, adult) aggression that places our loyalties firmly on the side of the alien – despite him being, when all is said and done, an ugly little brute with arms reminiscent of the monsters that tried to destroy Earth in *The War of the Worlds*. If we were in the same position, we would expect our own kind to be sympathetic. And here Spielberg disarms any of our potential lack of sympathy with a creature so ugly by making him small, vulnerable, isolated, large-eyed and innocent – just as we all were, or perceive ourselves to have been – when we were children. E.T. is a child lost from its parents, and whatever it looks like, it deserves our sympathy for that. 'Throughout,' said Spielberg,

> E.T. was conceived by me as love story – the love between a 10-year-old boy and a 900-year-old alien. In a way I was terrified. I didn't think I was ready to make this movie – I had never taken my shirt off in public before. But I think the result is a very intimate, seductive meeting of minds.

The emotional loading in E.T.'s favour is compounded by the brilliant design of the creature (created by Carlo Rambaldi, who replaced Rick Baker, allegedly following a row with Spielberg over costs and scheduling), which makes him seem like an ugly but helpless puppy dog, plus the fact that all he really wants to do is to get back to his own kind. Spielberg described the genesis of his idea for the creature:

> When I was first deciding whether E.T. should be a boy or a girl, big or small, happy or sad, I went through a book, looking at great men's and women's eyes. I did a compilation drawing of Carl Sandburg, Ernest Hemingway and Albert Einstein – from forehead to nose. Then I went to a lot of other books and found pictures of newborn infants. Taking the scissors, I cut out the eyes of Carl Sandburg and pasted them over the face of a small child. And I remember saying to myself, 'That is weird!' And Carlo Rambaldi took it from there.

Three E.T. models were in fact made for a total of $700,000 for which Spielberg received a mass of electronic equipment beneath layers of fibreglass and latex rubber. Rambaldi, the designer of Dino de Laurentis' 1976 *King Kong*, described how the first model was mechanical and bolted to the floor and had 30 points of movement in the face and 30 more in the body. The second, an auto-electronic model, had 86 separate points of movement. A third, capable of only ten movements, was cableless and designed for walking scenes. When, on the rare occasions none of the three models proved sufficiently 'human' enough – about 15 per cent of screen time – Pat Bilon, Tamara de Treaux and Mathew de Merritt (12 years old and legless since birth, though this was not publicized at the time) donned E.T. suits with electronic arms. Four additional heads were used to compliment other special effects devised by Lucas's Industrial Light and Magic Company.

The essence of E.T.'s plight is that he is marooned on Earth, and a victim of its environment. The longer he stays, the more ill he becomes, starved of the company of his own kind. Spielberg had wanted a creature 'that only a mother could love', ugly in appearance but with beauty in its character. His situation is in fact only made more palatable by the children – who are the only people who really understand his predic-ament – who ally with the extra terrestrial in an attempt to allow him the freedom to return to where he really belongs. To starve him of this right is to kill him. This situation, Spielberg hoped, would mean that the combination of his personality and his situation would help audiences to suspend any reservations they might have about flaws in his mechanical structure as some observers had with 'Bruce' in *Jaws*. Because E.T. was to be on-screen much longer than 'Puck' in *CE3K* had been, he needed not only Rambaldi's genius but Spielberg himself also needed to be at his very best in terms of choreography and editing.

It worked on all counts. *E.T.* was released in America in the summer of 1982 at roughly the same time as *Poltergeist*, with which it was perhaps inevitably compared. '*Poltergeist* is a scream,' said Spielberg, '*E.T.* is a whisper.' Together, claimed *Time* magazine, 'they re-establish the movie screen as a magic lantern, where science plays tricks on the eye as an artist enters the heart and nervous system with images that bemuse and beguile.'

5

Epilogue: Spielberg, Peter Pan and 'Hook'

American audiences, primed by four months of marketing hype, eagerly awaited the Christmas 1991 release of Spielberg's latest film, *Hook*. Spielberg had by then assumed a status which not only made his films ideal for the peak family viewing holiday season but also his older ones were considered ideal for prime time television scheduling. Almost a decade after *E.T.*, the film he was born to make (and in which Spielberg has the mother reading the Peter Pan story to her children), fans anticipated what promised to be Spielberg's ultimate autobiographical project: the long promised sequel to the Disney animated classic, *Peter Pan*, with a star-studded cast and a story about the boy who would not grow up, but who had in fact grown up. It was the film Spielberg – and Spielberg alone – had to make.

Others, however, had long since nurtured similar ideas. Andrew Birkin, author of *J. M. Barrie and the Lost Boys* which was turned into an acclaimed BBC television trilogy in the early 1980s, had attracted the interest of Francis Ford Coppola, who considered making a factional film about Barrie's relationship with the children who had inspired the original story. When Coppola ran into financial trouble, the idea was offered to Paramount who wanted Spielberg to direct it, and it was during this period, in the mid-1980s, that he began drafting his ideas. Then, without any real public explanation, Spielberg dropped the project – a decision not unconnected with the birth of his son Max – and instead he donated $1 million to Great Ormond Street Hospital in London, which had received the original copyright at Barrie's bequest. Spielberg said:

> My son took away my lost childhood and then he gave it back to me. When he was born I suddenly became the spitting image of my own father, with

all the parental clichés – all the things I swore I would never say to my own children.

Fifty years after Barrie's endowment, however, the copyright had supposedly expired. When the Disney studio attempted to claim the rights for itself, actor Mel Ferrer had successfully challenged the claim in the mid-1960s. Following Spielberg's withdrawal, Birkin then approached Columbia, where fellow Englishman David Puttnam had just taken over, but although he liked the idea, he was not prepared to assume the enormous preparatory costs that Spielberg had incurred at Paramount. The copyright issue remained a legal quagmire. Puttnam was then deposed, whereupon American producer Jerry Weintraub entered the fray with British producer Dodi Fayed, encouraged by Great Ormond Street Hospital, which needed the funds from any profits made by any film.

Hook screenwriter Jim V. Hart explained the film's genesis: 'For years we've been trying to come up with a sequel to *Peter Pan* – everybody in the business has.' In 1982, his then two-year-old son Jake drew a picture of a crocodile eating Captain Hook but reassured his father that it hadn't really happened. Hart continued:

> So for four years I walked around going, 'Captain Hook's not dead, he could get the perfect revenge – but where's the story?' So now Jake is six years old, and at the dinner table we play a family game of 'What if?'. And then Jake said the magic words: 'What if Peter Pan grew up?'

After various rewrites, producers Craig Baumgarten and Gary Adelson finally sold the screenplay to Mike Medavoy at TriStar Pictures, formerly Columbia and now owned by the Sony Corporation. Nick Castle was earmarked to direct it but then Amblin Entertainment, which of course had long been interested in a Peter Pan film, moved in. According to Kathleen Kennedy:

> We worked on a screenplay, spent quite a bit of time in development, and over a period of time came to the conclusion that it was a movie that in many respects Steven had already made in his mind, and certainly through some of his other work.

Spielberg said:

> What got to me about this new version of a grown-up Pan who has forgotten what it is like ever to have been a child, is that a lot of people today are losing their imagination because they are so driven by work, and the children in the family become almost incidental.

Castle was replaced as director by Spielberg, who was approached again, reportedly on Dustin Hoffman's suggestion. Amidst rumours of 'difficult negotiations' leading to a financial settlement, to avoid any further acrimony, and because Spielberg was hesitant about replacing a fellow director (being 'horrified' when he discovered Castle's attachment to the project), Medavoy took the responsibility for informing the original director. Castle was co-credited for *Hook*'s 'screenstory'. Also apparently on Hoffman's suggestion, Malia Scotch Marmo was recruited to strengthen the title character that Hoffman would be playing, which turned out to be like a Terry-Thomas character with an affected British accent in a Charles II wig. 'He plays it like a cross between Ronald Colman and James Mason', said a fellow actor.

Filming in the first half of 1991 proved hard work for the cast and crew (especially for Julia Roberts who was at one point admitted to hospital following her much publicized split with former fiancé, Kiefer Sutherland) although their labours were lightened by the rapport which developed between Hoffman and Robin Williams. In the scene where Hook makes Peter walk the plank of the lavishly recreated 80 by 135 foot pirate ship the *Jolly Roger*, Williams fell into the water, Spielberg shouted 'action!' and three mermaids dived in to save him. Underwater loudspeakers played the shark theme from *Jaws*, whereupon Williams surfaced, yelling: 'There's an agent in the water – and he wants his 10 per cent.' Such stories emerged only after the filming was completed as part of the pre-release publicity hype; the filming itself was shrouded in secrecy for fear that pages from the script would fall into the wrong hands.

Spielberg's choice of Julia Roberts, the Cinderella whore of *Pretty Woman* fame, was unusual. He explained:

> It is what Julia is in real life – which is a tomboy who walks kind of gawky-like and is accessible – that made me want her. She wasn't going to be an ephemeral fairy, a mystical creature. She was going to be a nuts-and-bolts, down-to-earth girl, which Julia is in real life.

Though much criticized for her performance, Roberts does in fact capture the flirtatiousness of the Tinkerbell character that is evident in Barrie's original story. She claimed to have drawn heavily upon her recent emotional traumas for her demanding (flying) role:

> What motivates Tinkerbell in *Hook* is this complete and hopeless love she has for Peter. It has gone on for all of time and that is something I can understand – she is his protector and his guide in a way, keeping him away from harm. She can understand when he refuses to understand who he really is. That does happen with men.

Peter (Robin Williams) rediscovering his childhood with the help of Jack (Charlie Korsmo), in *Hook*. Spielberg's most expensive film to date, panned by critics and loved by audiences.

In Spielberg's Neverland (as it has now become), Captain Hook has survived the crocodile which he has had stuffed and made into a giant clock which stands in the town square of the pirate village. The clock analogy is significant: 'We are all afraid, like Hook, of that big clock in our lives. And when you have kids, the clock goes faster', explained Spielberg who by now had four children (two of his own, with another on the way, one adopted and one stepdaughter). Hook discovers that the now grown-up Wall Street businessman Peter is flying to London – even though he hates flying on airplanes. In fact, the film was shot in Culver City, on the same stages used for the filming of *The Wizard of Oz*. On Peter's arrival to pay tribute to Wendy at a reunion dinner, Hook decides to kidnap Peter's children and, egged on by Smee (Bob Hoskins), to win over their affections as his revenge on his former adversary. Peter is forced to rescue his children, with the help of Tinkerbell and the distinctly punkish Lost Boys, in the process, rediscovering his youth, his flying skills and the lost love of his children. Bob Hoskins explained: '*Peter Pan* is about lost childhood. *Hook* is about lost fatherhood. If you take the child's love away from him, Pan the father becomes impotent.' 'It's an allegory for all of us adults', said Spielberg, who together with fellow fathers of young children, Hoskins, Williams and Hoffman, was drawing upon his parental hopes and fears to inject their personalities and experiences into the film to make it 'a tale of wonder and delight for children of all ages'. It was Speilberg's largest budget film to date, costing an astonishing $70–80 million (the exact figure has never been disclosed) – making it the second most expensive movie ever made.

Predictably, the fans loved it – with the film quickly beginning to recoup its costs over the holiday period and before its Royal British release at Easter 1992, although it was estimated that it would need to earn at least £120 million worldwide for it to recoup all its costs. Predictably, the critics expressed their reservations, with *Newsweek* comparing it to 'a huge party cake of a movie, with too much frosting'. The Disney associations with the Peter Pan story led to unfair comparisons with the 1953 classic not to mention the hugely successful recently released animated Disney feature, *Beauty and the Beast*.

Hook's commercial success was, however, according to Alexander Walker (for whom 'the child in me, I'm afraid, just threw up'), due to 'the perpetual American anxiety over the male menopause'. The storyline itself is an ingenious updating of the J.M. Barrie story, based upon the assumption that Peter Pan has in fact grown up to become a 40-year-old Wall Street businessman who has forgotten the joys of childhood, and is more interested in work than his own children. At 44, Spielberg was the same age as Barrie when Peter Pan was first produced as a play in 1904. Spielberg admitted to a high degree of directional identification with the character: 'I've always been Peter Pan. That's why I wanted to do this movie. In a way it's typecasting for me, because I've always felt a great affinity with that character.' Robin Williams felt likewise, having emerged from the drugs and divorce syndrome that afflicts many Hollywood personalities: 'I'd rather be the man who plays with his children and, in doing so, becomes a boy again sometimes. And you can have both, which is why *Hook* appeals to me so much.'

George Perry was one of the few critics to praise the film lavishly:

> Hook confirms that there has not been a filmmaker since Disney who has
> such an instinctive feeling for the rapture and the magic of a child's

imagination as Steven Spielberg. Quite simply, it is the best kids' film in many years. For adults, it probes recesses of the memory that have long been papered over. The special effects are naturally spectacular, but are only an element of the overall conception.

Nonetheless, most critics saw only the lavish sets and the special effects as being worthy of note, regarding the film as over-long, self-indulgent and shallow.

In 1985, following the release of his first supposedly adult film, *The Color Purple*, Spielberg had said:

> Yes, I'm growing up, but I think I am simply becoming an older Peter Pan. The one thing I don't want to lose is the fairy dust: I don't think any filmmaker can afford to lose that kind of magic.

And, he added,

> You have probably seen the most successful films I shall ever make, but I don't think you have seen the best of what I can do as a filmmaker.

Whether or not *Hook* eventually manages to recoup its huge costs, economic circumstances will probably dictate that most of Speilberg's future projects will have to be smaller, more intimate affairs. If he can recreate the formula employed in *E.T.* in his post-40 work, there is no reason why he should not prove as successful.

Penetrating Speilberg's own publicity machinery, it is possible to develop a picture of Spielberg as a hard-nosed businessman. Many agents fight shy of Amblin because the company devours so many projects without ever producing them, and many critics accuse Spielberg of meglomania. The problem is that he likes to be in total control of his projects and, in a multi-million dollar business, it is as well that the man who has proved most consistently successful in delivering profit-making goods retains almost autocratic power. Spielberg's next project is *Jurassic Park*, based on Michael Crichton's dinosaur/science fiction novel and, after that, the long-promised *Schindler's Ark* which may exorcize Spielberg's fascination with the Holocaust. But one thing is likely: if Spielberg can continue to develop his film characters – not only children – *and* concentrate on strong storylines derived from literary scripts whilst perhaps resisting the temptation to improvise quite so much, he may one day earn the Oscar he has long craved. After all, as Spielberg has pointed out: 'At the end of *Hook*, Peter has rescued his past – which is important for everyone who feels they have lost theirs.' Yet he is in no hurry to finally grow up: 'I'm not unhappy to be considered a maker of films which appeal to young people. I really do like being a children's storyteller.'

Filmography

Early television work, 1969–72

(Unless stated otherwise, the following were directed by Spielberg while working at Universal Studios for NBC television. Dates given are for first transmission.)

NIGHT GALLERY

Eyes (8 November 1969)

Teleplay: Rod Serling

Cast: Joan Crawford, Barry Sullivan, Tom Bosley

Joan Crawford plays a wealthy New York socialite who is going blind. She offers her fortune to a needy Tom Bosley in exchange for his eyes which will function only a few hours longer. The doctor, Barry Sullivan, performs the operation and later removes the bandages just as the lights go out in the 1965 East Coast blackout.

MARCUS WELBY

Daredevil Gesture (17 March 1970)

Cast: Robert Young, James Brolin, Elena Verdugo, Frank Webb, Marsha Hunt, Ronne Troup, Susan Albert, Peter Hobbs

Dr Welby treats a teenage haemophiliac.

NIGHT GALLERY

Make Me Laugh (6 January 1971)

Teleplay: Rod Serling

Cast: Godfrey Cambridge, Jackie Vernon, Tom Bosley, Al Lewis, Sidney Clute, John J. Fox

The story of a desperate comic who would do anything to raise a laugh and an equally desperate miracle worker who begins to doubt his powers.

THE NAME OF THE GAME

L.A. 2017 (15 January 1971)

Teleplay: Philip Wylie

Cast: Gene Barry, Barry Sullivan, Edmond O'Brien, Sharon Farrell, Severn Darden, Paul Stewart

Science fiction story about an ecological disaster facing Los Angeles in the 21st century.

THE PSYCHIATRISTS

The Private World of Martin Dalton (10 February 1971)

Teleplay: Bo May

Cast: Roy Thinnes, Jim Hutton, Kate Woodville, Stephen Hudis, Pamelyn Ferdin

Psychiatrist Roy Thinnes stumbles upon the deep secret behind the fantasy life into which the young Stephen Hudis has withdrawn because of parental hatred.

THE PSYCHIATRISTS

Par for the Course (10 March 1971)

Teleplay: Bo May, Thomas Y. Drake & Jerrold Freedman

Cast: Roy Thinnes, Clu Galager, Joan Darling, Michael C. Gwynne

Professional golfer Clu Galager is dying of cancer and is unable to cope with his fears until aided by his doctor and friends.

COLUMBO

Murder by the Book (15 September 1971)

Teleplay: Steve Bocho

Cast: Peter Falk, Jack Cassidy, Martin Milner, Rosemary Forsyth, Barbara Colby

The first ever series episode (as distinct from pilot TV movies) with the intrepid Peter Falk unravelling his raincoat and a murder by mystery writer Jack Cassidy who has plotted what he thinks is the perfect crime against his former collaborator, Martin Milner.

DUEL

(13 November 1971)
see below, under feature films as director

CBS FRIDAY NIGHT MOVIE

Something Evil (21 January 1972; Universal for CBS)

Teleplay: Robert Clouse

Cast: Sandy Dennis, Darren McGavin, Ralph Bellamy, John Rubinstein, Johnny Whittaker, Jeff Corey, David Knapp, Laurie Hagen, Sandy & Debbie Lempert

Family buys a Buck Country farm with a curse on it; a devil-possession story in which mother proves more than a match for her demonic adversary who attempts to possess her weird-looking son.

NBC WORLD PREMIERE

Savage (a.k.a. 'Watch Dog' and 'The Savage Report') (31 March 1972; 74 mins)

Screenplay: Barry Levison, William Link & Mark Rogers

Cast: Martin Landau, Barbara Bain, Will Geer, Barry Sullivan, Michelle Carey, Paul Richards, Louise Latham, Dabney Coleman, Pat Harrington

Supreme Court Nominee Barry Sullivan, taking time out from *Night Gallery* and *The Name of the Game*, finds himself compromised by blackmail photographs and TV journalists Landau and Bain try to find out why.

Feature films as director

(AA indicates Academy Award in one of the major categories)

DUEL

(1971, 74 mins, television; 1973, 85 mins, cinema) Universal Television Studios

Producer: George Eckstein; *Screenplay*: Richard Matheson (based on his published story); *Film editor*: Frank Moriss; *Director of photography*: Jack A. Marta; *Production Design*: Robert S. Smith; *Music*: Billy Goldenberg

Cast: David Mann (Dennis Weaver), Mrs Mann (Jacqueline Scott), Café Owner (Eddie Firestone), Bus Driver (Lou Frizzell), Man in Cafe (Gene Dynarski), Lady at Snakerama (Lucille Benson), Gas Station Attendant (Tim Herbert), Old Man (Charles Seel), Waitress (Shirley O'Hara), Old Man in Car (Alexander Lockwood), Old Woman in Car (Amy Douglass), Radio Interviewer (Dick Whittington), The Truck Driver (Cary Loftin), Car Driver (Dale Van Sickle)

A suburban travelling salesman is mysteriously menaced by an anonymous truck driver whose face is never seen and whose motives are never explained. The large, noisy, fume-emitting tanker contrasts with the neat ordered lifestyle of David Mann as symbolized by his orange-red company car. Car and truck play cat-and-mouse in what initially seems like harmless road fun. The car can obviously outrun the truck and Mann is at first relaxed. The truck becomes more aggressive, forcing Mann off the road at a local service stop. Mann tries to identify the truck driver at the service station but confronts the wrong man. Later he is flagged down by the driver of a broken-down schoolbus that needs a nudge start. The truck reappears and Mann flees, only to see the truck obligingly pushing the bus in his rear-view mirror. At a gas station and snake farm Mann tries to phone the police but the truck attacks the phone booth and he only just escapes. In a final showdown, after a close escape on a steep hill, Mann points his car at the truck and heads straight for it. He leaps from his car just before impact and watches as the truck plunges over a precipice. Mann dances a jig of relief as he watches the end of his enemy, brake fluid dripping like blood from the dying monster.

AVAILABLE IN UK FROM CIC VIDEO (PG)

THE SUGARLAND EXPRESS

(1973, 110 mins) Universal

Producers: Richard D. Zanuck & David Brown; *Screenplay*: Steven Spielberg, Hal Barwood, Mathew Robbins (from a story by Steven Spielberg); *Film Editors*: Edward M. Abroms, Verna Fields: *Director of Photography* (Panavision): Vilmos Zsigmond; *Production Design*: Joseph Alves; *Music*: John Williams

Cast: Lou Jean Poplin (Goldie Hawn), Clovis Poplin (William Atherton), Captain Tanner (Ben Johnson), Officer Slide (Michael Sacks), Officer Mashburn (Gregory Walcott), Baby Langston (Harrison Zanuck), Jessup (Steve Kanaly), Mrs Loony (Louise Latham), Mr Knocker (A.L. Camp), Mrs Knocker (Jessie Lee Fulton)

Lou Jean Poplin, newly-released from prison, helps her husband, Clovis, to escape from a remand centre so that they can liberate their son who has been placed in care by the Child Welfare Board because, as petty criminals, they have been declared unfit as parents. On their way to the foster home in Sugarland, Texas, they are pulled over by a highway patrolman for a routine check. Lou panics and grabs his gun and they take him hostage. They are pursued by the police and quickly become the focus of media attention. In the end they are shot by the pursuing police.

AVAILABLE IN UK FROM CIC VIDEO (PG)

JAWS

(1975, 124 mins) Universal

Producers: Richard D. Zanuck & David Brown; *Screenplay*: Peter Benchley, Carl Gottlieb (from the novel by Peter Benchley); *Film Editor*: Verna Fields (AA); *Director of Photography* (Panavision): Bill Butler; *Live shark footage*: Ron & Valerie Taylor; *Underwater Photography*: Rexford Metz; *Production Design*: Joseph Alves; *Special Effects*: Robert A. Mattey; *Music*: John Williams (AA). AA also for Sound (Robert L. Hoyt, Roger Herman, Earl Madery, John Carter)

Cast: Brody (Roy Scheider), Hooper (Richard Dreyfuss), Quint (Robert Shaw), Ellen Brody (Lorraine Gary), Vaughn (Murray Hamilton), Meadows (Carl Gottlieb), Hendricks (Jeffrey C. Kramer), Chrissie (Susan Backlinie), Cassidy (Jonathan Filley), Michael Brody (Chris Rebello), Sean Brody (Jay Mello), Estuary victim (Ted Grossman), Mrs Kintner (Lee Fierro), Alex Kintner (Jeffrey Voorhees), Ben Gardner (Craig Kingsbury), Medical examiner (Dr Robert Nevin), Interviewer (Peter Benchley).

The film opens with an attack by an unseen amphibious killer on a swimming girl. The next morning the girl's body is examined by Police Chief Brody, an ex-New Yorker who has fled to the relative calm of the tourist resort of Amity Island. The cause of death is confirmed as a shark attack. Brody tries to have the beaches closed but is opposed by town officials and businessmen. A second victim is claimed by the shark and it is decided to close the beach for 24 hours. A reward is offered for the capture of the shark. A shark is caught but Matt Hooper of the Oceanographic Institute examines it and decides that it is too small to be the right one. He explains to the mayor that there is a great white shark off the island but the mayor refuses to take on board the gravity of the situation and the beaches stay open. Following another attack Brody forces the mayor to hire Quint, a foul-mouthed veteran shark-hunter, to kill the shark. Quint, Brody and Hooper go after the shark in Quint's boat. The shark circles the boat and the three men begin to work together as a team to deal with the 25-foot, three-ton great white. The shark attacks the boat, denting the hull and damaging the engine. Hooper descends into the water in a shark cage in an attempt to fire a poison spear into the animal's mouth. He barely escapes with his life as the shark tears the cage to pieces. The shark then attacks the boat, killing Quint. Brody manages to dispatch the shark by exploding an oxygen cylinder that he has jammed in its mouth. Hooper and Brody head for shore.

AVAILABLE IN UK FROM CIC VIDEO (PG)

CLOSE ENCOUNTERS OF THE THIRD KIND

(1977, 135 mins; Special Edition re-release, 1980, 132 mins) Columbia

Producers: Julia & Michael Phillips; *Screenplay*: Steven Spielberg; *Film Editor*: Michael Kahn; *Director of Photography* (Panavision): Vilmos Zsigmond (AA); *Additional Photography*: William A. Fraker, Douglas Slocombe, John Alonzo, Laszlo Kovacs; *Production Design*: Joe Alves; *Special Effects*: Dougas Trumball; *Music*: John Williams
Special AA also for Sound Effects Editing (Frank Warner)

Cast: Roy Neary (Richard Dreyfuss), Claude Lacombe (François Truffaut), Ronnie Neary (Teri Garr), Jillian Guiler (Melinda Dillon), Barry Guiler (Cary Guffey), David Laughlin (Bob Balaban), Project Leader (J. Patrick McNamara), Wild Bill (Warren Kemmerling), Farmer (Roberts Blossom), Jean Claude (Philip Dodds), Brad Neary (Shawn Bishop), Silvia Neary (Adrienne Campbell), Toby Neary (Justin Dreyfuss), Robert (Lance Hendricksen), Team leader (Merill Connally), Major Benchley (George Dicenzo), Implantee (Alexander Lockwood), Implantee (Amy Douglas), Ike (Gene Dynarski), Mrs Harris (Mary Gafrey), Ohio Tolls (Norman Bartold), Larry Butler (Josef Sommer), Self (Rev Michael J. Dyer), Highway Patrolman (Roger Ernest), Military Police (Carl Weathers), ARP Project member (F.J. O'Neil), ARP Musician (Phil Dodds), Returnee 1 (Randy Hermann), Returnee 2 (Hal Barwood), Returnee 3 (Mathew Robbins)

An international team, led by Lacombe, has assembled in the Sonora Desert, Mexico, to investigate the return of a squadron of American aircraft that had been reported missing in 1945. The planes are in pristine condition but there is no sign of the crews. At Air Traffic Control, Indianapolis, a UFO encounter is monitored. Young Barry Guiler's toys start to move of their own accord in his suburban home in Muncie, Indiana. Elsewhere in Muncie, power company engineer Roy Neary is called out to attend to a power failure. As he stops to consult his map he is scanned by a flying object. With others, including Barry Guiler and his mother, Jillian, he witnesses a group of brightly-lit spaceships being pursued by police cars. In some excitement Roy drags his family out of bed and to the place where he had seen the lights. His face has been sunburned on one side. His behavious begins to grow erratic – his wife is upset and confused by her husband's experience. In northern India Lacombe witnesses a vast crowd of people chanting a five-note sequence. He learns that the sounds were heard from the sky. A group of scientists realize that they are receiving the co-ordinates of Devil's Mountain in Wyoming. Roy Neary has become obsessed by the vision of a mountain and has built a huge model. His wife and children leave him. Barry Guiler plays the five-note sequence on his xylophone. He is 'taken' by the aliens. Neary finally learns where his mountain is when he sees it on a television news item concerning an evacuation because of a chemical weapons incident. This is a ruse concocted by the military who want to clear the area of the civilian populace. Neary travels to Devil's Mountain where he meets Jillian Guiler who has been moved by the same vision. They are intercepted by soldiers in chemical warfare suits. They manage to escape with another man who has been driven there by his vision.

He falls victim to helicopter-sprayed sleeping gas but Roy and Jillian make it to the top of the mountain. There, they discover a huge scientific complex has been assembled. They watch as the scientists signal to a cluster of small spacecraft with the five-note sequence. Without warning the giant mothership appears, seeming to dwarf the mountain. Neary descends to the landing site. The mothership and the earth computers communicate through an exchange of musical phrases. Following this a ramp opens in the mothership and a number of people who have gone missing over the years emerge. These include the airforce crew whose planes were found in Mexico and Barry Guiler. Neary is led on board the mothership by the aliens and it ascends majestically into the sky.

AVAILABLE IN UK FROM RCA VIDEO (PG)

1941

(1979, 118 mins) Columbia/Universal/A-Team

Producer: Dean Edward Mitzner; *Executive Producer*: John Milius; *Screenplay*: Robert Zemeckis, Bob Gale (from a story by Zemeckis, Gale and Milius); *Film Editor*: Michael Kahn; *Director of Photography* (Panavision): William A. Fraker; *Production Design*: Dean Edward Mitzner; *Special Effects*: A.D. Flowers; *Visual Effects Supervisor*: Larry Robinson; *Music*: John Williams

Cast: Sergeant Tree (Dan Aykroyd), Ward Douglas (Ned Beatty), Wild Bill Kelso (John Belushi), Joan Douglas (Lorraine Gary), Claude (Murray Hamilton), Von Kleinschmidt (Christopher Lee), Birkhead (Tim Matheson), Commander Mitamura (Toshiro Mifune), Maddox (Warren Oates), General Stilwell (Robert Stack), Sitarski (Treat Williams), Donna (Nancy Allen), Herbie (Eddie Deezen), Wally (Bobby DiCicco), Betty (Dianne Daye), Foley (John Candy), Ogden Johnson Jones (Frank McRae), Dennis (Perry Lang), Hollis Wood (Slim Pickens), Maxine (Wendie Jo Sperber), Scioli (Lionel Stander), Meyer Mishkin (Ignatius Wolfington), USO MC (Joseph P. Flaherty).

The film opens on the morning of 13 December 1941, a few days after the Japanese attack on Pearl Harbor. In an almost exact reproduction of the opening scene of *Jaws* a girl goes swimming naked in the ocean. (It is in fact the same actress, Susan Backlinie.) A Japanese submarine surfaces beneath her. The captain and his Nazi advisor emerge on deck and decide to attack Hollywood. Meanwhile, a fanatical zealot of an American pilot, Wild Bill Kelso, attempts to protect Hollywood from an American aircraft, incompetently piloted by Captain Birkhead, whose interest is otherwise engaged by his passenger, Donna, whose fetish is having sex while flying. On the coastline, an ordinary American family get caught up in the chaos of the submarine attack when it mistakes a fairground for Hollywood. The father destroys his own home in the process of repelling the attack. While all this is going on, the man in charge of protecting the city, Donna's boss General Stilwell, is busy watching *Dumbo* at the cinema.

AVAILABLE IN UK FROM CIC VIDEO (PG)

RAIDERS OF THE LOST ARK

(1981, 118 mins) Paramount/Lucasfilm

Producer: Frank Marshall; *Executive Producers*: George Lucas, Howard Kazanjian; *Screenplay*: Lawrence Kasdan (from a story by George Lucas & Philip Kaufman); *Film Editor*: Michael Kahn (AA); *Director of Photography* (Panavision): Douglas Slocombe; *Production Design*: Norman Reynolds, Leslie Dilley (AA); *Visual Effects*: Richard Edlund, Kit West, Bruce Nicholson, Joe Johnston (AA); *Associate to Mr Spielberg*: Kathleen Kennedy; *Music*: John Williams AA for Best Sound Editing (Varney et al); Special AA for Sound Effects (Ben Burtt et al)

Cast: Indiana Jones (Harrison Ford), Marion (Karen Allen), Belloq (Paul Freeman), Toht (Ronald Lacey), Sallah (John Rhys-Davies), Satipo (Alfred Molina), Dietrich (Wolf Kahler), Gobbler (Anthony Higgins), Brody (Denholm Elliott), Barranca (Vic Tablian), Col. Musgrove (Don Fellows), Major Eaton (William Hootkins), Bureaucrat (Bill Reimbold), Jock (Fred Sorenson), Australian Climber (Patrick Durkin), 2nd Nazi (Mathew Scurfield), Ratty Nepalese (Malcom Weaver), Mean Mongolian (Sonny Caldinez), Mohan (Anthony Chinn), Giant Sherpa (Pat Roach), Otto (Christopher Frederick), Imam (Tutte Lemkow), Omar (Ishaq Bux), Abu (Kiran Shah), Fayah (Souad Messaoudi), Monkey Man (Vic Tablian), Arab Swordsman (Terry Richards), Mr Ford's Stand-In (Jack Dearlove)

Indiana Jones leads a team of men through a South American jungle in 1936. They are following a map in search of a priceless treasure in the Temple of the Chachapoyan Warriors. One by one Indiana's companions vanish into the jungle. Escaping many perils, he reaches the relic but is forced to give it up into the hands of his arch-enemy, Belloq, and flee a band of marauding natives. In the next scene Indiana is in college in his role as professor of archaeology. His friend Marcus and two American military intelligence agents tell him of an intercepted Nazi communique – the Staff of Rah, key to finding the Ark of the Covenant, has been discovered near Cairo. Indiana is given the job of getting the Ark before the Nazis do. He flies to Nepal to buy a vital piece of the Staff from Marion Ravenwood, whose father found it years before. In Cairo they discover that Belloq is leading the Nazis' excavation. Amidst the confusion of an ambush in a bazaar Marion is kidnapped. Indiana realizes that the Nazis are digging in the wrong place for the Ark as they are missing the headpiece of the Staff, which he has. He discovers the right place to look, he also finds Marion but refuses to free her while he goes to find the Ark. He finds it in a pit full of snakes, the only thing he fears. As the Ark is being hauled out the Nazis discover him and take possession of the Ark – Indiana is left in the snake-pit, and Marion is thrown in with him. Indiana's resourcefulness gets them out; they discover that the Ark has been shipped out by truck and set off in pursuit. After a chase, friendly Arabs help Indiana, Marion and the Ark to escape aboard a pirate steamer.

They are intercepted by a German U-boat. Marion and the Ark are captured and Indiana swims after them, somehow managing to get on board the submarine. Disguised as a German soldier he follows the Ark to a Greek island where Belloq and the Nazis open it. Supernatural forces emerge, melting the Nazis in a sea of fire

LA-2396

Harrison Ford and Karen Allen star in *Raiders of the Lost Ark*, 1981.

but leaving Indiana and Marion unscathed. Back in Washington the Ark is packed into a crate marked Top Secret and stored in a huge warehouse full of identical crates.

AVAILABLE IN UK FROM CIC VIDEO (PG)

E.T. – THE EXTRA TERRESTRIAL

(1982, 115 mins) Universal

Producers: Steven Spielberg, Kathleen Kennedy; *Screenplay*: Melissa Matheson (from an idea by Steven Spielberg); *Film Editor*: Carol Littleton; *Director of Photography*: Allan Daviau; *Production Design*: James D. Bissell; *Visual Effects Supervisor*: Dennis Muren (AA, with Kenneth F. Smith); *Production Supervisor*: Frank Marshall; *Associate Producer*: Melissa Matheson; *Production Manager*: Wallace Worsely; *Special*

Effects Coordinator: Dale Martin; *Music*: John Williams
AA for Best Sound Recording (Robert Knudson, Robert Glass, Don Digirolamo, Gene Cantamessa); AA for Best Sound Effects (Charles L. Campbell, Ben Burtt)
ET Design: Carlo Rambaldi (AA); *ET's Voice Design*: Ben Burtt; *ET Technical Supervisor*: Steve Townsend; *Additional ET Effects*: RobertShort; *ET Eyes Design*: Beverley Hoffman; *ET Movement Coordinator*: Caprice Rothe; *ET Operators*: Robert Avila, Eugene Crum, Frank Schiefler, Bob Townsend, Steve Willis, Richard Zarro, Ronald Zarro, Pat Billon, Tamara de Treaux, Mathew De Meritt, Tina Palmer, Nancy MacLean, Pam Ybarra.

Cast: Elliott (Henry Thomas), Mary (Dee Walace), Keys (Peter Coyote), Michael (Robert MacNaughton), Gertie (Drew

Barrymore), Greg (H.C. Martel), Steve (Sean Frye), Tyler (Tom Howell), Pretty Girl (Erika Elenian), Schoolboy (David O'Dell), Science Teacher (Richard Swingler), Policeman (Frank Toth), Ultra Sound Man (Robert Baton), Van Man (Michael Darrell)

An alien is accidentally left behind when his spaceship has to make an emergency take off from Earth. He is befriended by Elliott, a lonely young boy.

In the surrounding hills men are searching for the alien using electronic equipment. In the house ET shows Elliott and his brother and sister where he comes from, using levitated fruit to demonstrate. Later, ET formulates his plan to 'phone home' after watching SF films on television.

Gertie, Elliott's sister, tries to introduce ET to her mother, but the mother is too preoccupied to see or hear the alien. When Elliott returns home, ET, speaking to him for the first time, tells him of his desire to go home. Elliott smuggles ET into the forest on Hallowe'en night to set up his communication equipment. He reassures ET that time will be needed for the answer to come. ET is growing ill, however, he must return home to survive. ET goes missing and Elliott returns home distraught. His brother Michael finds ET dying in a stream and manages to get him home, despite being pursued by scientists. Elliott is ill, too, and the children have to take their mother into their confidence. Suddenly, the house is invaded by faceless scientists in protective suits. The house is converted into a research laboratory.

The scientists try to save ET but he appears to die, severing his telepathic contact with Elliott as he does so. Grief-stricken, Elliott makes his farewells to his friend. But ET revives and Elliott's grief becomes joy. Michael and Elliott steal the ambulance carrying ET. More children set up a diversion on their bicycles. ET is transferred to a bicycle basket and the children escape from pursuing police cars when ET levitates the bicycles over a roadblock. In the forest the spaceship returns and ET at last 'goes home'.

AVAILABLE IN UK FROM CIC VIDEO (U)

INDIANA JONES AND THE TEMPLE OF DOOM

(1984, 118 mins) Paramount/Lucasfilm

Producer: Robert Watts; *Executive Producers*: George Lucas, Frank Marshall; *Screenplay*: Willard Huyck & Gloria Katz (based on a story by Lucas); *Film Editor*: Michael Kahn; *Director of Photography* (Panavision): Douglas Slocombe; *Production Design*: Elliot Scott; *Visual Effects*: Dennis Muren, Michael McAlister, Lorne Peterson, George Gibbs (AA); *Music*: John Williams

Cast: Indiana Jones (Harrison Ford), Willie Scott (Kate Capshaw), Short Round (Ke Huy Quan), Mola Ram (Amrish Puri), Chattar Lal (Roshan Seth), Capt. Blumburtt (Philip Stone), Lao Che (Roy Chiao), Shaman (D.R. Nanayakkaru), Chieftain (Dharmadasa Kuruppu), Wu Han (David Yip), Kao Kan (Ric Young), Little Maharajah (Raj Singh), Chief Guard (Pat Roach)

Indiana Jones teams up in Shanghai with nightclub singer Willie Scott. He is trying to exchange a Manchu dynasty urn for a large diamond payment from Lao Che but is double-crossed by the Chinese gangsters and drugged with a deadly poison. In an elaborate set-piece fight, Indiana tries to get the antidote while Willie tries to get the diamond. Indy and the girl leap from the window and are saved by Short Round, a young boy older than his years. At the airport all three board a plane for Siam, only to discover in flight that it is Lao Che's plane. Lao Che's men parachute to safety leaving them to crash. They abandon ship in an inflatable raft, which ends up in river rapids.

Indiana and his companions arrive at a village that has been cursed since the local Maharajah confiscated its sacred protective stone. The crops have withered, the animals have died and the children have vanished. Indiana gets involved in saving the village. They travel to the Maharajah's palace. He turns out to be a thirteen-year-old boy.

That night, after Indy has escaped a would be assassin's attack, they make their way into the Temple of Doom. Here a Thuggie ceremony is underway at which the Maharajah is present. A human sacrifice is called for and a priest plucks out the heart of a caged man. The stone stolen from the village is placed inside a rock skull where it starts to glow. Indiana thinks this may be caused by diamonds, when he goes down into the chamber to get them Short Round and Willie are discovered and captured. Indy finds enslaved zombie children mining in the caves. He is also captured and reunited with Shorty. The high priest explains that the children are looking for two more stones. Indiana is forced to drink the zombie fluid. Shorty is sent to work in the mines – and Willie is to be the next sacrifice. She is placed in a cage and lowered into the pit. Shorty breaks free and brings Indiana back to his senses. He manages to haul Willie out of the pit. The three escape via the mines.

Indiana encourages the children to revolt. Pursued by the Thuggies, the three flee in a mining truck, emerging from a cliff-face just ahead of a giant wave of water released by the Thuggies. They head for a bridge. On the bridge Shorty and Willie are recaptured. By cutting the ropes that hold the bridge, Indiana sends most of their attackers to their doom in the alligator-infested waters below. Indiana manages to wrest control of one of the stones from the priest, who is torn to pieces by the alligators. The stone is returned to the village – and the children to their mothers and fathers.

AVAILABLE IN UK FROM CIC VIDEO (PG)

THE COLOR PURPLE

(1985, 150 mins) Warner Bros/Amblin

Producers: Steven Spielberg, Kathleen Kennedy, Frank Marshall & Quincy Jones; *Executive Producers*: Jon Peters & Peter Guber; *Screenplay*: Menno Meyjes (based on the novel by Alice Walker); *Film Editor*: Michael Kahn; *Director of Photography*: Allen Daviau; *Production Design*: J. Michael Riva; *Special Effects Supervisor*: Matt Sweeney; *Music*: Quincy Jones

Cast: Mister/Albert Johnson (Danny Glover), Celie (Whoopi Goldberg), Shug Avery (Margaret Avery), Sofia (Oprah Winfrey), Harpo (Willard Pugh), Nettie (Akosua Busia), Young Celie (Desreta Jackson), Old Mr (Adolph Caesar), Squeak (Rae Dawn Chong), Miss Millie (Dana Ivey), Pa Johnson (Leonard Jackson), Grady (Bennett Guillory), Preacher (John Patton Jnr), Reverend Samuel (Carl Anderson), Corrine (Susan Beaubian), Buster (James Tillis), Mayor (Phillip Strong), Swain (Larry Fishburne), Adam (Peto Kinbaka), Olivia (Lelo Masamba), Odessa (Margaret Freeman), Young Harpo (Howard Starr), Young Olivia (Daphaine Oliver), Young Adam (Jadili Johnson), Young Tashi (Lilian Njoki Distefano), Daisy (Donna Buie), Store Clerk (Leon Rippy), Mailman (John R. Hart), Road Gang Leader (David Thomas), Loretta (Carrie Murray)

Two sisters, Celie and Nettie, play pattycake happily in a field of purple flowers. Celie keeps house for Mister, to whom she has been given by her incestuous father. Mister treats her like a slave. When Mister makes advances towards Nettie she rejects him and he throws her out. He forcefully separates the two sisters, throwing stones at Nettie to keep her away.

As Mister's ill treatment of Celie continues, her only escape is found in reading. Mister, unknown to Celie, confiscates Nettie's letters to her. Harpo,

Mister's oldest son, falls in love with and marries the formidable Sofia. At first, Harpo is happy to be dominated by Sofia, but male peer pressure and, ironically, advice from Celie, force him to beat her. Sofia fights back and leaves him, her fighting spirit intact. When she and her children are patronized in town by Miss Millie, the Mayor's wife, who asks Sofia to come and work for her, Sofia replies 'Hell, no.' Her refusal to apologize leads to Sofia being arrested and jailed. When she is released, badly beaten, she is forced to work for Miss Millie after all.

Harpo converts their house into a drinking saloon. Shug Avery, who is recuperating from illness at Mister's house, will perform here after she has recovered. Celie and Shug strike up a friendship. Shug's femininity and independence contrast with Celie's servility. Shug sings an ode to Celie at Harpo's saloon, the prelude to her courtship of her. When Shug goes to Memphis, Celie has to stay behind but she has learned a little defiance.

When Shug returns several years later she is married. While her husband and Mister get to know each other, Shug collects the letters from the mailman. One of them is to Celie from her sister. Celie learns that her sister is now raising her (Celie's) children in Africa. The women find all the earlier letters in Mister's room. As she reads the letters over the next few weeks she learns of Nettie's adventures in an African missionary school and that she is coming home soon.

Sofia returns home just as Shug and her husband are about to leave, announcing that they will take Celie with them. Celie tells Mister exactly what she thinks of him. Sofia is roused by Celie's spirit. Harpo's girlfriend says she will also go to Memphis. Without Celie, Mister's home falls apart, he starts drinking and the farm starts going to ruin. Celie returns home for the funeral of her step-father. She inherits the house – which should have been hers by rights when her real mother and father died – and opens a shop selling elasticated trousers. Shug sings at Harpo's. Her voice interrupts a church service and as the choir try to drown out her voice she starts to sing gospel songs with them. She leads the people from Harpo's into the church – where she is accepted back into the fold by the preacher, her father.

Nettie returns, her return paid for by Mister, who is trying to make amends to Celie. There is an emotional reunion between the sisters and Celie's African-speaking children in the purple-coloured fields as Mister looks on.
AVAILABLE ON VIDEO IN UK FROM WHV (15)

EMPIRE OF THE SUN

(1987, 146 mins) Warner Bros/Amblin
Producers: Steven Spielberg, Kathleen Kennedy, Frank Marshall; *Executive Producer*: Robert Shapiro; *Screenplay*: Tom Stoppard (based on the novel by J.G. Ballard); *Film Editor*: Michael Kahn; *Director of Photography*: Allen Daviau; *Production Design*: Norman Reynolds; *Music*: John Williams

Cast: Basie (John Malkovich), Mrs Victor (Miranda Richardson), Dr Rawlins (Nigel Havers), Frank (Joe Pantaliano), Maxton (Leslie Phillips), Mr Lockwood (Robert Stephens), Lt. Price (Paul McGann), Jim Graham (Christian Bale), Sgt Naguta (Mabato Ibu), Jim's Mother (Emily Richard), Jim's Father (Rupert Frazer), Mr Victor (Peter Gale), Kamikazi Boy Pilot (Takatoki Kataoka), Dainty (Ben Stiller), Tiptree (David Neidorf), Cohen (Ralph Seymour), Yang (Zhai Nai She), Amy Mathews (Emma Piper)

The film begins in the International Settlement at Shanghai on the eve of Pearl Harbor, December 1941. A wealthy British couple and their 11-year-old son, Jamie, go to a fancy dress ball. Jamie is fascinated by aeroplanes. He is growing up in a war-torn world and fantasizes as much about flying them as playing with them as toys. Jamie's father takes the family into a hotel. Playing with his toys by flashlight, Jamie signals to a warship in the harbour, which returns the signal before opening fire. 'I didn't mean it,' says the boy as his father takes him to the evacuation point where all is chaos.

A pitched street battle erupts and amidst the confusion Jamie is separated from his parents. He returns home to find the house is being looted by servants. Jamie stays until the food supplies run out and then leaves on his bicycle. He tries to surrender to some Japanese soldiers making a propaganda film but they just mock him. He is taken by an American truckdriver to a dockside house where another American, Basie, examines his teeth and his possessions before rechristening him Jim. He takes the Americans to his old house where lights make him think that his mother has returned. Actually, the house is being used as a Japanese officers' retreat and Basie is beaten up.

Jim wakes with a fever in a prison camp. Basie has worked out the rules of the place and teaches the boy a few rudimentary survival tricks. Jim escapes from the camp in a truck when he is able to show the Japanese driver that he understands where he is going on the map. They arrive at a work camp and Jim is immediately instructed to carry rocks. Examining a fighter plane under repair, Jim salutes three airmen who return the salute. The next days he watches a Japanese boy playing with a toy glider and they exchange greetings.

By 1945, Jim is the camp survivor, wheeling and dealing, swapping and stealing. His adoptive parents are tiring of the strange boy and insist he moves into the single men's dormitory. An American bomber crashes just outside the camp. Several Japanese soldiers want to attack the American airmen in the hospital. The doctor who tries to stop them is beaten. Jim remonstrates with the Japanese officer, reminding him, in Japanese, of his dignity. Dressed in baseball cap and sunglasses, Jim is very much part of the American set-up.

One morning, Jim watches a ritual Kamikaze ceremony. He salutes the pilots and sings with them in Japanese. Suddenly there is an American air attack. Jim dashes backwards and forwards, eventually collapsing into a dazed state as the doctor takes him to his foster parents. The next day the camp is evacuated. Jim throws his suitcase full of mementoes into the river. He stays to watch his foster mother die. As he wanders across the wasteland he hears the news of the atomic bombs and the surrender of Japan. Basie kills the Japanese boy whom Jim had earlier befriended when he thinks the boy is trying to kill Jim. Basie and his cronies drive off, leaving Jim bicycling around the camp. He surrenders to arriving American troops. In a giant glass conservatory Jim is reunited with his parents.

AVAILABLE ON VIDEO IN UK FROM WHV (15)

INDIANA JONES AND THE LAST CRUSADE

(1989) Paramount/Lucasfilm

Executive Producers: George Lucas, Frank Marshall; *Screenplay*: Jeffrey Boam (from a story by Lucas and Menno Meyjes); *Film Editor*: Michael Kahn; *Director of Photography*: Douglas Slocombe; *Production Design*: Elliot Scott; *Visual Effects Supervisor*: Michael J. McAllister; *Music*: John Williams

Cast: Indiana Jones (Harrison Ford), Professor Henry Jones (Sean Connery), Marcus Brody (Denholm Elliott), Elsa (Alison Doody), Sallah (John Rhys-Davies), Walter Donovan (Julian Glover), Young Indy (River Phoenix), Vogel (Michael Byrne), Kazim (Kevork Malikyan), Grail Knight (Robert Eddison), Fedora (Richard Young), Sultan (Alexei Sayle), Young Henry (Alex Hyde-White), Panama Hat (Paul Maxwell), Mrs Donovan (Mrs Glover), Butler (Vernon Dobtcheff), Herman (J.J. Hardy), Roscoe (Bradley Gregg), Half Breed (Jeff O'Haco).

Rough Rider (Vince Deadrick), Sheriff (Mark Miles), Deputy Sheriff (Ted Grossman), Young Panama Hat (Tim Hiser), Scout Master (Larry Sanders), Scout No. 1 (Will Miles), Scout No. 2 (David Murray)

The film begins in Utah, 1912. A troop of scouts are exploring caves when two of them come across some gold-diggers led by a fedora-wearing man. One of the scouts is the young Indiana Jones. Realising its significance, Indiana grabs the 16th-century cross the treasure hunters have dug up and flees on his horse. The thieves pursue him in cars. He mounts a circus train and is chased from boxcar roof to boxcar roof. He falls into the snake car and is covered by them. This is the origin of Indiana's fear of snakes. He scrambles out only to fall into the lion car. He fends the beast off with a whip but cuts his face in the process. Eventually he hides in a magician's trunk and mysteriously gets off the train. His adversary smiles in admiration as the train pulls away. Back home, the sheriff arrives with the thieves and makes Indiana hand over the cross. The leader hands Indiana his fedora. In the next scene the adult Indiana Jones is about to be thrown overboard from a steamer and is forced to hand over the cross again to the same pursuers. After a struggle he jumps into the sea and the boat explodes.

Later, outside the college where he teaches, he is approached by three men who take him to the home of millionaire Walter Donovan. Here he is shown an engraving that is a clue to the whereabouts of the Holy Grail. Donovan wants the eternal life the grail promises. He needs Indiana's help because the project leader, Indiana's father, Henry, has disappeared.

Professor Jones's house has been ransacked, Indiana's only clue to his whereabouts is a package posted from Venice. Flying there with Marcus, he meets Dr Elsa Schneider, his father's German assistant, who takes him to a

library in a converted church. From notes in his father's diary, Indiana finds the tomb of a Grail knight in the library. They find the second marker to the Grail but have to flee when pursuers set fire to the chamber. The pursuers are members of a society dedicated to protecting the Grail's secret. Indiana finds out from one of them that his father is being held in a castle on the Austro-German frontier. Indiana and Elsa go to Grunewald castle – he realizes it is a Nazi operation. He meets up with his father and the two men bring each other up to date on the situation. They are interrupted by the Nazis who demand the diary. It emerges that Elsa is a Nazi. She is summoned back to Berlin. Escaping from the castle, Indiana and his father follow her. In Berlin, they succeed in retrieving the diary, even having it autographed by Hitler in the process! They leave Germany in a zeppelin but when they realize that it is turning round to fly back they flee in its escape plane and are pursued by a German fighter. They crashland into a house and steal a car. Finally they shake off their pursuers when a flock of seagulls fly into the path of a pursuing plane.

The Sultan of Hatay offers his services to the Nazis. In Hatay, the Joneses meet up with Sallah, who explains that the Nazis are ahead in the desert, following the map that will lead them ot the Grail. They intercept the Nazi convoy, helped by members of the Grail protection society. There is a skirmish, but the Nazis arrive at the Canyon of the Crescent Moon ahead of them. The Joneses' party are captured. Donovan shoots Henry, thus forcing Indiana to attempt to negotiate the traps that surround the Grail in order to obtain its healing power. He succeeds, reaching a chamber where he finds the last Grail knight. Donovan and his party follow. From a number of chalices, Donovan chooses the wrong one and disintegrates into dust. Indiana makes the right choice and Henry is healed. Elsa attempts to escape with the Grail but the ground opens beneath her and she falls to her death. Henry tells Indiana to leave the Grail where it has fallen. They escape outside as the temple collapses around them.

AVAILABLE ON VIDEO IN UK FROM CIC (PG)

ALWAYS

(1989, 117 mins) Universal/Amblin

Producers: Steven Spielberg, Frank Marshall, Kathleen Kennedy; *Screenplay*: Jerry Belson (from Dalton Trumbo's screenplay of *A Guy Named Joe* (1943) from a story by Chandler Sprague and David Boehm, adapted by Frederick Hazlitt Brennan); *Film Editor* (Panavision): Michael Kahn; *Director of Photography*: Mikael Salomon; *Production Design*: James Bissell; *Music*: John Williams

Cast: Peter Sandich (Richard Dreyfuss), Dorinda Durston (Holly Hunter), Brad Johnson (Ted Baker), Al Yackey (John Goodman), Hap (Audrey Hepburn), Ted Baker (Brad Johnson), Dave (Robert Blossoms), Powerhouse (Keith David), Nails (Ed Van Nuys), Rachel (Marg Helgenberger), Fire Boss (Dale Dye), Alex (Brian Haley), Charlie (James Lashly), Grey (Michael Steve Jones)

The first part of the film establishes the love affair between Pete, a legendary pilot flying B26s on firefighting missions, and Dorinda. Al, a fellow pilot, thinks Peter is a 'dickhead' because he takes unnecessary risks bombing fires. Pete and Dorinda row over her desire to fly and his reluctance to quit and live a quiet life training pilots. Eventually he agrees but goes on one last flight to fight a forest fire. Al gets into trouble but Pete manages to save him at the cost of his own life. An angel called Hap explains to Pete that he is being sent back to give inspiration to others, especially pilots and particularly Ted Baker, who has been pursuing Dorinda. It is six months later. No one can see or hear Pete when he returns to learn that Al and Dorinda have left, he to work in a training school, she to mourn Pete.

Al takes Dorinda back to Flat Rock. During a routine flight, accompanied by the ghost of Pete, a storm forces Ted to land. He encounters an old hobo who can actually hear Pete. Pete talks to Ted through the hobo. Pete coaches Ted subliminally in the art of flying but he still has to endure Ted's courtship of Dorinda. Ted saves the life of a schoolbus driver, which gains him favour with Dorinda – and Pete. Ted begins to assume more and more of Pete's characteristics, which leads to Dorinda becoming more attracted to him.

Hap returns to remind Pete that his life is over, but gives him the chance to say goodbye to Dorinda so that they both can be free. A serious forest fire breaks out and Ted takes it upon himself to help. Dorinda takes a plane up herself. Pete helps her, but she does all right. The shared close experience allows Pete to release her. They crash into a lake and Dorinda is prepared to let herself die but Pete saves her. Finally he moves out of her heart and she is free to go off with Ted.

AVAILABLE ON VIDEO IN UK FROM CIC (PG)

HOOK

(1991, 135 mins) Sony Pictures Entertainment/Tristar Pictures/Amblin

Executive Producer: Jim V. Hart; *Producers*: Kathleen Kennedy, Frank Marshall, Gerald R. Molen; *Screenplay*: Jim V. Hart, Malia Scotch Marmo; *Screenstory*: Jim V. Hart, Nick Castle; *Designer*: Norman Garwood; *Music*: John Williams

Cast: Hook (Dustin Hoffman), Peter Banning (Robin Williams), Tinkerbell (Julia Roberts), Smee (Bob Hoskins), Rufio (Dante Basco), Peter's son, Jack (Charlie Korsmo), Maggie (Amber Scott), Moira Banning (Caroline Goodall), Pirate (Glenn Close), Wendy (Maggie Smith), Policeman (Phil Collins)

Peter Blanning (Robin Williams) has grown up into an angst-ridden but successful businessman who hates to fly and has blocked out his memories of being Peter Pan. Yet he is invited to London to speak in tribute to Wendy (Maggie Smith) and to celebrate her lifelong dedication to orphans, whereupon his children are kidnapped by Captain Hook (Dustin Hoffman) and taken to Never Never Land. There, encouraged by Smee (Bob Hoskins) and his pirate crew (including a difficult-to-spot Glenn Close), Hook befriends Peter's children in an attempt to woo their affections away from their father who, with the aid of Tinkerbell (Julia Roberts), goes to rescue his children and in the process rediscovers his childhood innocence, his flying skills – and the love and respect of his own children.

Feature films as producer/ executive producer

I WANNA HOLD YOUR HAND

(1978, 104 mins) Universal

Director: Robert Zemeckis; *Executive Producer*: Steven Spielberg; *Producers*: Tamara Asseyev, Alex Rose; *Screenplay*: Robert Zemeckis, Bob Gale; *Director of Photography*: Donald M. Morgan; *Production Design*: Peter Jamison; *Film Editor*: Frank Morriss; *Music*: The Beatles

Cast: Nancy Allen, Bobby Di Cicco, Mark McLure, Susan Kendall Newman, Theresa Saldana, Wendie Jo Sperber, Eddie Deezen, Christian Jutner, Will Jordan, Read Morgan, Claude Earl Jones, James Houghton, Michael Hewitson

A comedy about six New Jersey teenagers who try to infiltrate the Ed Sullivan show on the night the Beatles first appeared.

USED CARS

(1980, 107 mins) Columbia

Director: Robert Zemeckis; *Executive Producer*: Steven Spielberg; *Producer*: Bob Gale; *Screenplay*: Robert Zemeckis, Bob Gale; *Director of Photography*: Donald M. Morgan; *Film Editor*: Michael Kahn; *Music*: Patrick Williams

Cast: Kurt Russell, Jack Warden, Gerrit Graham, Frank McCrae, Deborah Harmon, Joseph P. Flaherty, David L. Lander, Michael McKean, Michael Talbott, Harry Northop, Alfonso Arau, Al Lewis, Woodrow Partrey

Two used car dealers (Kurt Russell and Jack Warden) go to any lengths they can to attract customers in this zany and sometimes grotesque comedy.
AVAILABLE ON VIDEO IN UK FROM RCA/ COLOMBIA PICTURES VIDEO (RCA) (15)

CONTINENTAL DIVIDE

(1981, 103 mins) Universal

Director: Michael Apted; *Producer*: Bob Larson; *Executive Producer*: Steven Spielberg; *Screenplay*: Lawrence Kasdan; *Director of Photography*: John Bailey; *Film Editor*: Dennis Virkler; *Music*: Michael Small

Cast: John Belushi, Blair Brown, Allen Goorwitz, Carlin Glynn, Tony Ganios, Val Avery, Liam Russell, Everett Smith, Bill Henderson, Bruce Jarchow, Eddie Schwartz, Harold Holmes, Elizabeth Young

A romantic comedy about a hard-nosed journalist (John Belushi) who invades the mountain retreat of a reclusive scientist who dedicates herself to preserving wildlife (Blair Brown).
AVAILABLE ON VIDEO IN UK FROM CIC VIDEO (PG)

POLTERGEIST

(1982, 114 mins) Metro Goldwyn Mayer/ SLM

Director: Tobe Hooper; *Producers*: Steven Spielberg, Frank Marshall; *Associate Producer*: Kathleen Kennedy; *Screenplay*: Steven Spielberg, Michael Grais, Mark Victor; *Story*: Steven Spielberg; *Director of Photography*: Mathew F. Leonetti; *Production Designer*: James H. Spencer; *Film Editor*: Michael Kahn; *Visual Effects Supervisor*: Richard Edlund; *Music*: Jerry Goldsmith

Cast: Jobeth Williams, Craig T. Nelson, Beatrice Straight, Dominique Dunne, Oliver Robbins, Heather O'Rourke, Michael McManus, Virginia Kiser, Martin Casella, Richard Lawson

A suburban family home is invaded via the television set by hostile supernatural entities which kidnap the five-year-old daughter. Renowned for its special effects, this horror/adventure yarn traces the trapping of the young girl in another dimension, the son being attacked by a tree and coffins and corpses rising from the swimming pool, and a monstrous demon.
AVAILABLE ON VIDEO IN UK FROM MGM/VA HOME VIDEO (15)

THE TWILIGHT ZONE – THE MOVIE

(1983, 101 mins) Warner Bros

Executive Producer: Frank Marshall; *Producers*: Steven Spielberg, John Landis; *Narrators*: Burgess Meredith, Dan Aykroyd, Albert Brooks

A homage to one of Spielberg's favourite television series, this four-episode movie (three of which are based on the television series) is a mixed bag, and Spielberg's contribution is about how old people in a rest home rediscover their youth with the aid of a travelling magician (Scatman Crothers).

Prologue and Segment One

Director & Screenplay: John Landis; *Director of Photography*: Stevan Larner; *Film Editor*: Malcolm Campbell; *Music*: Jerry Goldsmith

Cast: Dan Aykroyd, Albert Brooks, Vic Morrow, Doug McGrath, Charles Hallahan, Steven Williams, Annette Claudier, Stephen Bishop, Joseph Hieu, Albert Leong

Segment Two: 'Kick the Can'

Director: Steven Spielberg; *Screenplay*: George Clayton Johnson, Richard Matheson, Josh Rogan; *Director of Photography*: Allan Daviau; *Film Editor*: Michael Kahn; *Music*: Jerry Goldsmith

Cast: Scatman Crothers, Bill Quinn, Martin Garner, Selma Diamond, Helen Shaw, Murray Matheson, Peter Brocco, Priscilla Pointer

Segment Three: 'It's a Good Life'

Director: Joe Dante; *Screenplay*: Richard Matheson (from a story by Jerome Bixby); *Director of Photography*: John Hora; *Film Editor*: Tina Hirsch; *Music*: Jerry Goldsmith

Cast: Kathleen Quinlan, Jeremy Licht, Kevin McCarthy, Patricia Barry, William Schallert, Nancy Cartwright

Segment Four: 'Nightmare at 20,000 Feet'

Director: George Miller; *Screenplay*: Richard Matheson (from his own story); *Director of Photography*: Allen Daviau; *Film Editor*: Howard Smith; *Music*: Jerry Goldsmith

Cast: John Lithgow, Abbe Lane, Donna Dixon, John Dennis Johnston, Larry Cedar, Charles Knapp, Christina Nigra, Lonna Schwab
AVAILABLE ON VIDEO IN UK FROM WARNER HOME VIDEO (15)

GREMLINS

(1984, 106 mins) Warner Bros/Amblin

Director: Joe Dante; *Executive Producers*: Steven Spielberg, Frank Marshall, Kathleen Kennedy; *Producer*: Michael Finnell; *Screenplay*: Chris Columbus; *Director of Photography*: John Hora; *Production Design*: James H. Spencer; *Film Editor*: Tina Hirsch; *Music*: Jerry Goldsmith; *Gremlins Creator*: Chris Walas

Cast: Zach Galligan, Phoebe Cates, Hoyte Axton, Polly Holliday, Francis Lee McCain, Judge Reinhold, Keye Luke, Don Steele, Scott Brady, Arnie Moore, Corey Feldman, Dick Miller, Glynn Turman, Jonathan Banks, Edwards Andrews

A whimsical morality tale with some very

Gremlins, 1984, one of numerous films produced by Spielberg's Amblin Entertainment Company in the 1980s, making the stamp 'Steven Spielberg' a hallmark of commercial success.

dark moments in a film that successfully combines horror, comedy and fairy tale. When enthusiastic inventor (Hoyt Axton) brings home a cuddly, wide-eyed little creature he names 'Gizmo' as a Christmas present for his son (Zach Galligan), the trouble begins when he is exposed to water, sunlight and feeding after midnight, resulting in hideous murderous offspring which begin to terrorise the town in between revelling in *Snow White and the Seven Dwarves* at the local cinema. Spielberg appears briefly in this film stuffed with film references and jokes. AVAILABLE ON VIDEO IN UK FROM WARNER HOME VIDEO (15)

THE GOONIES

(1985, 111 mins) **Warner Bros/Amblin**

Director: Richard Donner; *Producers*: Richard Donner, Harvey Bernhard; *Executive Producers*: Steven Spielberg, Frank Marshall, Kathleen Kennedy; *Screenplay*: Chris Columbus; *Story*: Steven Spielberg; *Director of Photography*: Mike McLean; *Production Designer*: J. Michael Riva; *Film Editor*: Michael Kahn; *Music*: Dave Grusin

Cast: Sean Astin, Josh Brolin, Jeff Cohen, Corey Feldman, Kerri Green, Martha Plumpton, Ke Huy Quan, John Matuszak, Robert Davi, Joe Pantoliano, Anne

Ramsey, Lupe Ontivaros, Mary Ellen Trainer, Keith Walker, Curtis Hanson, Steve Antin, Paul Tuerpe

An adventure tale about a group of youngsters in Oregon who, in attempting to save their parents' homes from land developers, discover a pirate treasure map and go in search of the treasure, travelling through dark and dangerous caves before finding the splendidly recreated pirate ship.

AVAILABLE ON VIDEO IN UK FROM WARNER HOME VIDEO (PG)

BACK TO THE FUTURE

(1985, 116 mins) Universal/Amblin

Director: Robert Zemeckis; *Executive Producers*: Steven Spielberg, Kathleen Kennedy, Frank Marshall; *Producers*: Bob Gale, Neil Canton; *Screenplay*: Robert Zemeckis, Bob Gale; *Director of Photography*: Dean Cundy; *Production Design*: Lawrence G. Paull; *Film Editor*: Arthur Schmidt, Harry Keramidas; *Music*: Alan Silvestri; *Special Effects*: Steven Suits, Kimberley Pike, Sam Adams, Richard Chronister, William Klinger, Neil Smith & David Wischnack
AA for Best Sound Effects (Charles L. Campbell/Robert Rutledge)
AA for Best Sound Effects (Charles L. Campbell/Robert Rutledge)

Cast: Michael J. Fox, Christopher Lloyd, Lea Thompson, Crispin Glover, Thomas F. Wilson, Claudia Wells, Marc McClure, Wendie Jo Sperber, George DiCenzo

A time travel comedy adventure in which a teenager (Michael J. Fox) becomes involved with a zany scientist (Christopher Lloyd) who has developed a De Lorean sports car into a time machine. Fox is whisked back to 1955 in an effort to ensure that his mother and father fall in love to ensure his own procreation. Some delightful period pieces combine with an attempt to overcome the paradoxes of time travel.

AVAILABLE ON VIDEO IN UK FROM CIC (PG)

YOUNG SHERLOCK HOLMES

(1985, 109 mins) Paramount/Amblin
AKA *Young Sherlock Holmes and the Pyramid of Fear*

Director: Barry Levinson; *Executive Producers*: Stephen Spielberg, Frank Marshall, Kathleen Kennedy; *Producer*: Mark Johnson; *Screenplay*: Chris Columbus; *Director of Photography*: Stephen Goldblatt; *Production Design*: Norman Reynolds; *Film Editor*: Stu Linder; *Music*: Bruce Broughton

Cast: Nicholas Rowe, Alan Cox, Sophie Ward, Anthony Higgins, Nigel Stock, Susan Fleetwood, Freddie Jones, Michael Hordern, Earl Rhodes, Brian Oulton, Roger Ashton-Griffith, Patrick Newell, Donald Eccles, Matthew Ryan, Jonathan Lacey

An action adventure which cast Sherlock Holmes and Watson as students who solve a mystery in the true Conan Doyle tradition but who find themselves engaged in an Indiana Jones type adventure, of which it almost becomes a remake in its final part.

AVAILABLE ON VIDEO IN UK FROM CIC (PG)

THE MONEY PIT

(1986, 91 mins) Universal/Amblin

Director: Richard Benjamin; *Executive Producers*: Steven Spielberg, David Giler; *Producers*: Frank Marshall, Kathleen Kennedy, Art Levinson; *Screenplay*: David Giler; *Director of Photography*: Gordon Willis; *Film Editor*: Jacqueline Cambas; *Music*: Michael Colombier

Cast: Tom Hanks, Shelley Long, Alexander Goudenov, Maureen Stapleton, Joe Mantegna, Philip Bosco, Josh Mostel, Yakov Smirnoff, Carmine Caridi, Brian Backer, Billy Lombardo, Mia Dillono, John Van Dreelen, Douglas Watson

Virtually a remake of *Mister Blanding Builds his Dream House*, this comedy has a young couple (Tom Hanks and Shelley

Long) buying a fine house at a low price only to discover that it is falling apart and that it gobbles up all their savings and patience.

AVAILABLE ON VIDEO IN UK FROM CIC (15)

AN AMERICAN TAIL

(1986, 80 mins) Universal/Amblin

Director: Don Bluth; *Executive Producers*: Steven Spielberg, David Kirschner, Kathleen Kennedy, Frank Marshall; *Created by*: David Kirschner; *Producers*: Don Bluth, John Pomeroy, Gary Goldman; *Design and storyboard*: Don Bluth; *Screenplay*: Judy Freudbergh, Tony Geiss (from a story by David Kirschner, Judy Freudberg, Tony Geiss); *Directing Animators*: John Pomeroy, Dan Kuenster, Linda Miller; *Animators*: Lorna Pomeroy, Skip Jones, Gary Perkovac, Kevin Wurzer, Jeff Etter, Dave Spafford, Ralph Zondag, Dick Zondag, Dave Molina, Jesse Cosio, Heidi Guedel, Ralph Palmer, Anne Marie Barwell, T. Daniel Hofstedt; *Film Editor*: Dan Molina; *Music*: James Horner

Cast: (Voices of) Cathianne Blore, Dom DeLuise, John Finnegan, Phillip Glasser, Amy Green, Madeline Kahn, Pat Musick, Nehemiah Persoff, Christopher Plummer, Neil Ross, Will Ryan, Hal Smith, Erica Yohn

A full-length animated feature set in the 19th century in which a young Russian mouse, Feivel, becomes separated from his family as they arrive in America and which pursues his subsequent adventures.

AVAILABLE ON VIDEO IN UK FROM CIC (U)

INNERSPACE

(1987, 120 mins) Warner Bros/Amblin/ Guber-Peters

Director: Joe Dante; *Producer*: Michael Finnell; *Executive Producers*: Steven Spielberg, Peter Guber, Jon Peters; *Co-Executive Producers*: Frank Marshall, Kathleen Kennedy; *Co-Producer*: Chip Proser; *Screenplay*: Jeffrey Boam, Chip

Proser (based on a story by Chip Proser); *Director of Photography*: Andrew Laszlo; *Production Design*: James H. Spencer; *Film Editor*: Kent Beyda; *Music*: Jerry Goldsmith

AA Best Visual Effects (Dennis Muren/ William George/Harley Jessup/ Kenneth Smith)

Cast: Dennis Quaid, Martin Short, Meg Ryan, Kevin McCarthy, Fiona Lewis, Henry Gibson, John Hora, Robert Picardo, Wendy Schaal, William Schallert, Harold Sylvester, Mark L. Taylor, Vernon Wells

Comedy adventure in which a Navy test pilot (Dennis Quaid) is miniaturised as part of a test experiment only to find his submarine-like vehicle accidentally injected into the bloodstream of a hypochondriac supermarket worker instead of the intended laboratory rabbit.

AVAILABLE ON VIDEO IN UK FROM WARNER HOME VIDEO (PG)

BATTERIES NOT INCLUDED

(1987, 106 mins) Universal

Director: Mathew Robbins; *Executive Producers*: Steven Spielberg, Kathleen Kennedy, Frank Marshall; *Producer*: Robert L. Schwartz; *Screenplay*: Brad Bird, Mathew Robbins, Brent Maddock, S.S. Wilson (from a story by Mike Garris); *Associate Producer*: Gerald R. Molen; *Director of Photography*: John McPherson; *Production Design*: Ted Haworth; *Film Editor*: Cynthia Scheider; *Music*: James Horner

Cast: Hume Cronyn, Jessica Tandy, Frank McRae, Elizabeth Pena, Michael Carmine, Denis Boutsikaris, Tom Aldridge, Jane Hoffman, John Disanti, John Pankow, MacIntyre Dixon, Michael Greene, Doris Belack, Wendy Schaal, James LeGros, Jose Santana

A group of tenants about to be evicted from their building that is scheduled for demolition find some unexpected mechanical assistance from tiny but

friendly aliens who pay them a visit.
AVAILABLE ON VIDEO IN UK FROM CIC (PG)

WHO FRAMED ROGER RABBIT?

(1988, 105 mins) Touchstone/Amblin

Director: Robert Zemeckis; *Executive Producers*: Steven Spielberg, Kathleen Kennedy; *Producers*: Robert Watts, Frank Marshall; *Screenplay*: Jeffrey Price, Peter S. Seaman (from the book by Gary K. Wolf); *Director of Photography*: Dean Cundey; *Film Editor*: Arthur Schmidt (AA); *Music*: Alan Silvesti; *Director of Animation*: Richard Williams (AA) with Roger Cain; *Visual Effects Supervisor*: Ken Ralston (AA with Edward Jones); *Mechanical Effects Supervisor*: George Gibbs (AA)
AA for Best Sound Effects (Charles L. Campbell/Louis L. Edemann)

Cast: Bob Hoskins, Christopher Lloyd, Joanna Cassidy, Stubby Kaye, Alan Tilvern, Richard L. Parmentier, Voice of Roger: Charles Fleischer, Voice of Baby Herman: Lou Hirsch, Voice of Benny the Cab: Charles Fleischer, Jessica's Performance model: Betsy Brantley, Uncredited voice of Jessica: Kathleen Turner

A state-of-the-art mixture of live action and animation which sees a 1940s style PI (Hoskins) become involved in a murder investigation in 'Toontown' – where many of the leading cartoon characters of the past live and work for Hollywood studios – assisted by the chief suspect, Roger Rabbit.
AVAILABLE ON VIDEO IN UK FROM TOUCHSTONE HOME VIDEO (PG)

BACK TO THE FUTURE II

(1989, 105 mins) Universal/Amblin

Director: Robert Zemeckis; *Executive Producers*: Steven Spielberg, Kathleen Kennedy, Frank Marshall; *Producers*: Bob Gale, Neil Canton; *Director*: Robert Zemeckis; *Screenplay*: Bob Gale (from a story by Bob Gale, Robert Zemeckis);

Director of Photography: Dean Cundey; *Production Design*: Rick Carter; *Film Editors*: Arthur Schmidt, Harry Keramidas; *Associate Producer*: Steve Starkey; *Visual Effects Supervisor*: Ken Ralston; *Music*: Alan Silvestri

Cast: Michael J. Fox, Christopher Lloyd, Lea Thompson, Thomas F. Wilson, James Tolkan, Jeffrey Weissman, Casey Siemaszko, Billy Zane, J.J. Cohen, Charles Fleischer

Michael Fox, returning for the sequel, plays three different characters to go forward to the year 2015, back to 1955 and staying in the present – in another effort to resolve the time paradox.
AVAILABLE ON VIDEO IN UK FROM CIC (PG)

DAD

(1989, 108 mins) Universal/Amblin

Director: Gary David Goldberg; *Executive Producers*: Steven Spielberg, Frank Marshall, Kathleen Kennedy; *Producers*: Joseph Stern, Gary David Goldberg; *Co-producers*: Sam Weisman, Ric Kidney; *Screenplay*: Gary David Goldberg (based on the novel by William Wharton); *Director of Photography*: Jan Kiesser; *Production Design*: Jack DeGovia; *Film Editor*: Eric Sears; *Music*: James Horner

Cast; Jack Lemmon, Ted Danson, Olympia Dukakis, Kathy Baker, Kevin Spacey, Ethan Hawke

Guilt-ridden businessman (Ted Danson) reluctantly forced to care for his ageing father (Jack Lemmon), whereupon they rediscover their love and respect for each other through a series of adventures.
AVAILABLE ON VIDEO IN UK FROM CIC (U)

BACK TO THE FUTURE III

(1990, 105 mins) Universal/Amblin

Director: Robert Zemeckis; *Executive Producers*: Steven Spielberg, Kathleen Kennedy, Frank Marshall; *Producers*: Bob Gale, Neil Canton; *Screenplay*: Robert Zemeckis, Bob Gale; *Director of*

Photography: Dean Cundey; *Production Design*: Rick Carter; *Editor*: Arthur Schmidt, Harry Keramidas; *Music*: Alan Silvestri, ZZ Top

Cast: Michael J. Fox, Christopher Lloyd, Mary Steenburgen, Thomas F. Wilson, Lea Thompson, Elizabeth Shue

Run-on third part of the trilogy, made concurrently with the second film, which sees Michael J. Fox back in the Wild West.

AVAILABLE ON VIDEO IN UK FROM CIC (PG)

GREMLINS II: THE NEW BATCH

(1990, 106 mins) Warner Bros/Amblin

Director: Joe Dante; *Executive Producers*: Steven Spielberg, Kathleen Kennedy, Frank Marshall; *Producer*: Michael Finnell; *Screenplay*: Charlie Haas; *Director of Photography*: John Hora; *Production Design*: James Spencer; *Film Editor*: Kent Beyda; *Music*: Jerry Goldsmith; *Gremlins and Mogwai effects supervised by*: Rick Baker (Co-Producer)

Cast: Zach Galligan, Phoebe Cates, John Glover, Robert Prosky, Robert Picardo, Christopher Lee, Haviland Morris, Dick Miller, Jackie Joseph, Gedde Wantanabe, Keye Luke, Howie Mandel (as voice of Gizmo), Tony Randall (as voice of Brain Gremlin)

The sequel sees 'Gizmo' and his villainous offspring again running riot – but this time in New York's 'Clamp Tower'; again full of wonderful film gags and self-parody with some genuine horror touches.

AVAILABLE ON VIDEO IN UK FROM WARNER BROS HOME VIDEO (PG)

JOE VERSUS THE VOLCANO

(1990, 101 mins) Warner Bro/Amblin

Director: John Patrick Shanley (debut); *Executive Producers*: Steven Spielberg, Kathleen Kennedy, Frank Marshall; *Producer*: Teri Schwartz; *Screenplay*: John Patrick Shanley; *Director of Photography*: Stephen Goldblatt;

Production Design: Bo Welch; *Film Editor*: Richard Halsey; *Music*: George Delerue

Cast: Tom Hanks, Meg Ryan, Lloyd Bridges, Amanda Plummer, Robert Stack, Ossie Davis, Abe Vigoda, Dan Hedaya

Fantasy-comedy in the style of the 1930s, in which a bored office worker (Tom Hanks) is told he is dying, whereupon he accepts an offer by a millionaire to lead out the rest of his life in luxury in exchange for his eventual sacrifice to a South Sea volcano.

AVAILABLE ON VIDEO IN UK FROM WARNER BROS HOME VIDEO (15)

ARACHNOPHOBIA

(1990, 105 mins) Hollywood Pictures/ Amblin

Director : Frank Marshall (debut); *Executive Producers*: Steven Spielberg, Kathleen Kennedy, Frank Marshall; *Producers*: Kathleen Kennedy, Richard Vane; *Screenplay*: Don Jakoby, Wesley Strick (from a story by Don Jakoby, Al Williams); *Director of Photography*: Mikael Salomon; *Production Design*: James Bissell; *Film Editor*: Michael Kahn; *Music*: Trevor Jones

Cast: Jeff Daniels, John Goodman, Julian Sands, Harley Jane Kozak, Stuart Pankin, Brian McNamara, Mark L. Taylor, Henry Jones, Mary Carver

Spiders go on the rampage.

AVAILABLE ON VIDEO IN UK FROM HOLLYWOOD PICTURES HOME ENTERTAINMENT (PG)

AN AMERICAN TAIL II : FIEVEL GOES WEST

(1991, 84 mins) Universal/Amblin

Directors: Phil Nibbelunk, Simon Wells; *Executive Producers*: Frank Marshall, Kathleen Kennedy, Steven Spielberg; *Producers*: Steven Spielberg, Robert Watts; *Screenplay*: Flint Dille; *Story*: Charles Swenson; *Creator*: David Kirshner; *Music*: James Horner (with original songs by Horner and Will Jennings)

More animated adventures for our Russian immigrant mouse, this time in the Wild West.

Later Television Work, 1985–7

AMAZING STORIES

Series Details:
Amblin/Universal

Executive Producer: Steven Spielberg; *Production Executives*: Kathleen Kennedy, Frank Marshall; *Producer*: David E. Vogel; *Developed by*: Steven Spielberg, Joshua Brand, John Falsey; *Supervising Producers*: Joshua Brand, John Palsey; *Associate Producers* (except when stated otherwise): Stephen Semel, Steve Starkey; *Story Editors*: Mick Garris, Peter Z Orton; *Production Designer*: Rick Carter; *Theme Music*: John Williams; *Creative Consultant*: Richard Matheson

THE MISSION

(1985)

Director: Steven Spielberg; *Teleplay*: Menno Meyjes (based on a Spielberg story); *Editor*: Steven Kemper; *Director of Photography*: John McPherson; *Music*: John Williams

Cast: Kevin Costner, Casey Siemaszko, Kiefer Sutherland, Jeffrey Jay Cohen, John Philbin, Gary Mauro, Glen Mauro

A World War Two bombing mission over Germany is in trouble when the belly gunner's turret is damaged, trapping the crew member and the landing gear is shot out. Excellent tension and period mood as Spielberg combines his lighting expertise with his love of aircraft – and his love of animation as the frantic trapped crew member literally paints himself out of a corner, drawing wheels onto a sketch that magically provides wheels for the plane to land.
AVAILABLE ON VIDEO IN UK ON *AMAZING STORIES 1* FROM CIC

MUMMY DADDY

(1985)

Director: William Dear; *Teleplay*: Earl Pomorantz (based on a Spielberg story); *Editor*: Joe Ann Fogle; *Director of Photography*: Robert Stevens; *Music*: Danny Elfman, Steve Bartek

Cast: Tom Harrison, Bronson Pinchot, Brion James, Tracey Walter, Larry Hankin, Luay Lee Flippin, William Frankfather, Arnold Johnson, Michael Zand

A comedy episode about an actor called Harold, playing the part of The Mummy in a film who is called away from the set to the birth of his child – still in costume. Driving through redneck country on his way to the hospital, his car runs out of petrol whereupon he is taken for a real monster and is hunted down by the locals. He takes refuge with a blind man who is housing the original Mummy that had terrorised the district back in the 1920s. Harold eventually reaches the hospital to become a daddy, while the real Mummy doubles for him back at the film set.
AVAILABLE ON VIDEO IN UK ON *AMAZING STORIES 1* FROM CIC

GO TO THE HEAD OF THE CLASS

(1985)

Director: Robert Zemeckis; *Teleplay*: Mick Garris, Tom McLouglin, Bob Gale (from a story by Garris); *Editor*: Wendy Greene Bricmont; *Director of Photography*: John McPerson; *Music*: Alan Silvestri

Cast: Christopher Lloyd, Scott Coffey, Mary Stuart Masterson, Tom Breznaha, Billy Beck

A fantasy story about school kids plotting revenge on their teacher, which gets out of control as they dabble in black magic.
AVAILABLE ON VIDEO IN UK ON *AMAZING STORIES 1* FROM CIC

THE AMAZING FALSWORTH

(1985)

Director: Peter Hyams; *Teleplay*: Mick Garris (based on a story by Spielberg); *Editor*: Steven Kemper; *Director of Photography*: Robert Stevens; *Associate Producers*: Skip Lusk, Stephen Semel, Steve Starkey; *Music*: Billie Goldenberg

Cast: Gregory Hines, Richard Masur, Don Calfa, Suzanne Bateman, Robert Lesser

A psychopathic killer is on the loose when a psychic magician establishes mental contact with him. There follows a tense hunt as the killer tries to murder him and he only survives with the help of a shotgun and his magical hands in the final confrontation.

AVAILABLE ON VIDEO IN UK ON *AMAZING STORIES 2* FROM CIC

GHOST TRAIN

(1985)

Director: Steven Spielberg; *Teleplay*: Frank Deese (based on a Spielberg story); *Editor*: Steven Kemper; *Director of Photography*: Allen Daviau; *Associate Producers*: Skip Lusk, Steve Starkey; *Music*: John Williams

Cast: Robert Blossoms, Scott Paulin, Gail Edwards, Lukas Haas, Ronny Roker

Spielberg plays with a full-size train set as a wise old grandfather prepares to board the ghost train that comes to collect the dying.

AVAILABLE ON VIDEO IN UK ON *AMAZING STORIES 2* FROM CIC

FINE TUNING

(1985)

Director: Bob Balaban; *Teleplay*: Earl Pomerantz (from a Spielberg story); *Associate Producers*: Steve Starkey, Skip Lusk; *Director of Photography*: Robert Stevens; *Editor*: Joe Ann Fogle; *Music*: Jonathan Tunick

Cast: Mathew Laborteaux, Gary Riley, Jimmy Gatherum, Milton Berle, Debbie Carrington, Daniel Frishman, Patty Maloney

A teenage science prodigy builds a television antenna capable of picking up transmissions from outer space. Aliens are monitoring 'I Love Lucy' and other classic American TV shows. Prodigy and his two friends discover that the aliens have launched an expedition to Earth and meet up with them in Hollywood, using the old NBC TV tune and the music from 'Bonanza' as mutual recognition of their friendship and joint culture. The aliens take them aboard their spaceship and they show them the Hollywood tourist sights, encountering Milton Berle in the process. The aliens are distraught that they will not go back to their planet with them, but the boys round up some ageing vaudevillians who will go back with them.

AVAILABLE ON VIDEO IN UK ON *AMAZING STORIES 8* FROM CIC

DOROTHY AND BEN

(1985)

Director: Thomas Carter; *Teleplay*: Michael de Guzman (based on a Spielberg story); *Editor*: Joe Ann Fogle; *Director of Photography*: John McPherson; *Music*: George Delerue

Cast: Joe Seneca, Lane Smith, Louis Giambalvo, Kathleen Lloyd, Joe Regalbuto, Natalie Gregory

A hospital patient miraculously recovers after forty years on a life-support machine and discovers he can communicate with a child in coma. He goes to death in her place.

AVAILABLE ON VIDEO IN UK ON *AMAZING STORIES 4* FROM CIC

THE MAIN ATTRACTION

(1985)

Director: Mathew Robbins; *Teleplay*: Brad Bird, Mick Garris (based on a

Spielberg story); *Editor*: Steven Kemper; *Director of Photography*: John McPherson; *Music*: Craig Safan

Cast: John Scott Clough, Lisa Jane Persky, Richard Bull, Barbara Sharma, Tom Napier, Bill Allen

A vain, spoiled high school jock is in a contest to sell the most Prom tickets when his house is hit by a meteor that magnetizes him – the girl he hates most is magnetized too and they are drawn together.
AVAILABLE ON VIDEO IN UK ON *AMAZING STORIES 4* FROM CIC

MIRROR, MIRROR

(1985)

Director: Martin Scorsese; *Teleplay*: Joseph Minion (from a Spielberg story); *Director of Photography*: Robert Stevens; *Film Editor*: Joe Ann Fogle; *Associate Producers*: Steve Starkey, Skip Lusk; *Music*: Michael Kamen

Cast: Sam Waterston, Helen Shaver, Dick Cavett, Tim Robbins, Dana Gladstone, Valorie Grear, Michael C. Gwynne, Peter Iacangelo

A horror story writer (Sam Waterston) at the peak of his career cannot be scared by anything until he returns home from an interview with Dick Cavett to see a mysterious caped figure in his house mirrors who is trying to kill him. Nobody else can see the knife-wielding assailant until his girlfriend (Helen Shaver) sees Waterston himself become the creature whereupon, having revealed himself as a monster, he does the right thing and leaps out of the window to his death. Spine chilling over-the-shoulder stuff from Scorsese.
AVAILABLE ON VIDEO IN UK ON *AMAZING STORIES 6* FROM CIC

MR MAGIC

(1985)

Director: Donald Petrie; *Teleplay*: Joshua

Brand, John Falsey; *Director of Photography*: John McPherson; *Editor*: Joe Ann Fogle; *Associate Producers*: Steve Starkey, Skip Lisk; *Music*: Bruce Broughton

Cast: Sid Caesar, Leo Rossi, Larry Gelman, Julius Harris, Tim Herbert, Eda Reiss Merin

An ageing magician (Sid Caesar) who is losing his touch and is making a fool of himself on stage finds an old pack of magic cards that do remarkable things and revive his act. A story about an old man who has seen better days but who refuses to quit until his magic flying cards provide him with a swansong his audiences will never forget.
AVAILABLE ON VIDEO IN UK ON *AMAZING STORIES 6* FROM CIC

ONE AMAZING NIGHT

(1985)

Director: Phil Joanou; *Teleplay*: Joshua Brand & John Falsey (from a Spielberg story); *Director of Photography*: John McPherson; *Editor*: Steven Kemper; *Music*: Thomas Newman

Cast: Douglas Seale, Pat Hingle, Gabriele Damon, Marvin McIntyre, Frances Bay, Stephen Lee, Joanne Welles

Father Christmas is on his rounds and is arrested as a burglar in a suburban home in which Santa's existence is acknowledged only as a pleasant fairy tale. The hard-hearted arresting officer thinks he is a cranky old man and throws Santa in jail, having doubted his existence since failing to get a raygun as a child. The boy springs Santa from jail and a car chase between the patrol cars and the sleigh ends with Santa taking off and dropping the raygun to an astonished policeman. A cross between *Miracle of 42nd Street* and *A Christmas Carol*.
AVAILABLE ON VIDEO IN UK ON *AMAZING STORIES 7* FROM CIC

THE WEDDING RING

(1986)

Director: Danny DeVito; *Teleplay*: Stu Krieger (based on a Spielberg story); *Editor*: Steven Kemper; *Director of Photography*: Robert Stevens; *Music*: Craig Safan

Cast: Rhea Perlman, Danny DeVito, Louis Giambalvo, Bernadette Birkett, David Byrd, Tracey Walter

Real-life husband and wife, DeVito and Perlman, in a separation and reconciliation drama set in a diner.
AVAILABLE ON VIDEO IN UK ON *AMAZING STORIES 2* FROM CIC

THE GREIBBLE

(1986)

Director: Joe Dante; *Teleplay*: Mick Garris (from a Spielberg story); *Director of Photography*: Robert Stevens; *Editor*: Steven Kemper, *Music*: John Addison

Cast: Hayley Mills, Dick Miller, Justin Mooney, Don McLeod, Frank Welker, Jim Jansen

A hideous, yet cuddly, horned and cow-eyed alien mysteriously appears to a suburban housewife during a storm-caused blackout and proceeds to eat every piece of junk in sight (including most of the household decor). Despite Hayley Mills' initial desire to get rid of the hungry beast she forms an affection for the creature that no one else can see until she discovers that it is a comic book character that disappears when her son returns home complaining that his bedroom possessions have been thrown out in the garbage – including his favourite greibble comic.
AVAILABLE ON VIDEO IN UK ON *AMAZING STORIES 3* FROM CIC

MISCALCULATION

(1986)

Director: Tom Holland; *Teleplay*: Michael McDowell; *Associate Producers*: Stephen Semel, Steve Starkey, Cheryl Bloch; *Director of Photography*: Charles Minsky; *Editor*: Joe Ann Fogle; *Music*: Phil Marshall

Cast: Jon Cryer, Joann Willette, Jeffrey Jay Cohen, Lana Clarkshon, Calyn Gorg, Catherine Gilmour, Elisabeth de Turenne, Rebecca Schaeffer, Wynonna Smith, Penelope Sudrow, Harry Woolf, Al Lampkin, Alden Milikan

A high school kid searching for a date spills some laboratory chemicals over a dog magazine and transforms the cover photograph into a real dog. He takes home a girly magazine and repeats the experiment but uses too much chemicals and produces a ten-foot-high nyphomaniac centrefold who destroys his bedroom before melting. He tries again using less chemicals – and produces an ugly skeletal fiend. The third time he produces a half torso. The fourth time works only for the girl to walk off with Phil's friend. The remaining chemicals spill onto a copy of *Fangoria* magazine . . . Bizarre stuff from the co-writer of *Beetlejuice*.
AVAILABLE ON VIDEO IN UK ON *AMAZING STORIES 3* FROM CIC

BLUE MAN DOWN

(1986)

Director: Paul Michael Glaser; *Teleplay*: Jacob Epstein, Daniel Lindley (from a Spielberg story); *Director of Photography*: Charles Minsky; *Editor*: John Wright; *Music*: Brad Fiedel

Cast: Max Gail, Kate McNeil, Chris Nash, Sal Viscuso, Eddie Zammit, Michael Villella, Frank Doubleday

Two patrol cops attend a supermarket robbery and the younger partner is killed due to the older man's incompetence. His new partner, a tough but jolly female (Kate McNeil), helps him to restore his confidence, especially in heroically avenging his partner's death by arresting the killer in a seige. He then discovers that his female partner is really the ghost of an officer who had been killed on a drug bust twelve years previously, and whose partner had committed suicide out of remorse.

AVAILABLE ON VIDEO IN UK ON *AMAZING STORIES 6* FROM CIC

THE 21 INCH SUN

(1986)

Director: Nick Castle; *Script*: Bruce Kirschbaum; *Director of Photography*: Robert Stevens; *Editor*: Joe Ann Fogle; *Music*: Ralph Burns

Cast: Robert Townsend, Michael Lerner, Craig Richard Nelso, Robert Starr, Bridget Sienna, Alan Solomon, Richard Chudnow

A comedy scriptwriter finding it difficult to come up with new material is offered an opportunity to write a comedy sit-com in one night. His house plants, cultivated by junk television and Billy's conversation, take over for him. An unlikely tale of rags to riches that works as it is played for laughs.

AVAILABLE ON VIDEO IN UK ON *AMAZING STORIES 7* FROM CIC

MAGIC SATURDAY

(1986)

Director: Robert Markowitz; *Script*: Richard Christian Matheson; *Director of Photography*: Robert Stevens; *Editor*: StevenKemper; *Music*: Ralph Burns

Cast: M. Emmet Walsh, Taliesin Jaffe, David Crowley, Caren Kaye, Jeff B. Cohen, David Arnott, David Donnely, Jeff A. Kinder

A young-at-heart old man is given the opportunity by his grandson to exchange bodies so that he can recapture his youth on the baseball field. While grandpa is winning new friends for the wimpish kid in the process, the boy discovers that he has inhabited a dying body and the race is on to get them restored to their proper places in time.

AVAILABLE ON VIDEO IN UK ON *AMAZING STORIES 7* FROM CIC

YOU GOTTA BELIEVE ME

(1986)

Director: Kevin Reynolds; *Teleplay*: Stu Krieger (from a Spielberg story); *Director of Photography*: Robert Stevens; *Editor*: Joe Ann Fogle; *Music*: Brad Fiedel

Cast: Charles Durning, Mary Betten, Ebbe Roe Smith, Wil Shriner, John Roselius, Jenie Sadler, Lance Nichols, Richard Burns, Gregory Wagrowski

Charles Durning is awoken abruptly in the night by a plane crash just outside his suburban home. It is a dream, but one so vivid he investigates further and ascertains that a plane carrying the people he has seen wandering about the wreckage is on a late night flight. No one believes his premonition so he takes matters into his own hands, ramming a light aircraft piloted by a drunk-driver who has strayed onto the wrong runway, thereby just saving the plane as it takes off.

AVAILABLE ON VIDEO IN UK ON *AMAZING STORIES 7* FROM CIC

THE DOLL

(1986)

Director: Phil Joanou; *Script*: Richard Matheson; *Director of Photography*: Robert Stevens; *Editor*: Steven Kemper; *Music*: Georges Delerue

Cast: John Lithgow, Annie Helm, Sharon Spelman, John Christopher Jones, Rainbow Phoenix, Albert Hague

A lonely bachelor (John Lithgow) is compelled to buy a doll, ostensibly for his niece, but finds himself falling in love with it. He discovers it is modelled on a lonely spinstress schoolteacher and calls upon her only to discover that she has also purchased a doll made in his likeness from the same doll-maker.

AVAILABLE ON VIDEO IN UK ON *AMAZING STORIES 5* FROM CIC

LIFE ON DEATH ROW

(1986)

Director: Mick Garris; *Teleplay*: Rockne

S. O'Bannon (from a story by Mick Garris); *Director of Photography*: Robert Stevens; *Editor*: Steven Kemper; *Music*: Fred Steiner

Cast: Patrick Swayze, James T. Callaghan, Kevin Hagen, Hector Elizondo, Nicholas Love, Hawthorne James, Arnold Johnson, Paul Eiding

A convicted killer (Patrick Swayze) awaiting his execution on death row joins a prison escape but is hit by lightning in the process. When he recovers, he discovers that he has acquired the power to heal the sick by touch but, despite efforts to get him repealed so that he can serve mankind by his unique gift, the execution goes ahead. As his body is wheeled from the electric chair, prisoners and guards realize that he is not dead and the show ends with the question 'What do we do now?'
AVAILABLE ON VIDEO IN UK ON *AMAZING STORIES* 5 FROM CIC

THANKSGIVING

(1986)

Director: Todd Holland; *Teleplay*: Pierre R. Debs, Robert C. Fox; *Director of Photography*: Charles Minsky; *Editor*: Steven Kemper; *Music*: Bruce Broughton

Cast: David Carradine, Kyra Sedgwick

A poor farming couple dig a well that breaks through to an underground community of 'hole people'. In return for hauling a torchlight down, gold is returned. As he rushes into town to buy more torchlights, she starts to lower food down with a greetings note and a dictionary, in return for which she is rewarded with jewellery and a note that reads 'Very tasty. Payment enclosed. What else do you have?' When the husband returns with a batch of cheap torchlights to lower, he is rewarded with their return, torn to pieces. Furious, he arms himself to the teeth and lowers himself down. When the wife hauls him up, his clothes are filled with riches but he is gone. The note reads: 'Our scholars

have determined that this food is turkey. Delicious. Payment enclosed. What else do you have?'
AVAILABLE ON VIDEO IN UK ON *AMAZING STORIES* 5 FROM CIC

THE PUMPKIN COMPETITION

(1986)

Director: Norman Reynolds; *Script*: Peter Z. Orton; *Director of Photography*: John McPherson; *Editor*: Wendy Greene Bricmont; *Music*: John Addison

Cast: Polly Holliday, June Lockhart, J.A. Preston, Ritch Brinkley, Britt Leach, Ann Walker, Joshua Rudoy

Moralistic story about meanness and selfishness in which a bitter, old, miserly spinster, sick of losing a pumpkin growing competition, is told a few home truths by the winner. A professor of agricultural science who has developed giant vegetables offers to help her win in return for research funding. She only gives him half of what he asks for but a giant pumpkin results. At the following year's competition, she wages her entire estate against the reigning champion, only to be defeated because the professor had also given his growth formula to the other competitors.
AVAILABLE ON VIDEO IN UK ON *AMAZING STORIES* 8 FROM CIC

WITHOUT DIANA

(1986)

Director: Lesli Linka Glatter; *Script*: Mick Garris; *Director of Photography*: John McPherson; *Editor*: Steven Kemper; *Music*: Georges Delerue

Cast: Billy Green Bush, Dianne Hull, Gennie James, Frederic Cook, Rick Andosca

Separation story in which a father, separated from his young daughter by the Second World War, attempts to overcome her resentment at him leaving his family. The girl is lost in the woods and he begins to understand his daughter's position as he and his wife await the results of the search party to no avail. In their old age, he again fears loneliness as his wife lies dying when his eight-year-old daughter returns unaged after forty years. She has returned to take her mother to heaven and reassure her father that the time will come for them all to be together again.

AVAILABLE ON VIDEO IN UK ON *AMAZING STORIES 8* FROM CIC

MOVING DAY

(1987)

Director: Robert Stevens; *Script*: Frank Kerr; *Director of Photography*: Vincent Martinelli; *Editor*: Suzanne Pettit; *Music*: David Shire

Cast: Stephen Geoffreys, Dennis Lipscomb, Mary Ellen Trainor, Kristen Vigard, Bill Wesley

A typical Spielberg-like middle-American teenage boy discovers from his father, whom he thinks is an inventor, that his parents are an alien observation team who now have to move on to a new assignment on a new planet. The boy's apprehensive anxiety is alleviated by the discovery that

his school sweetheart is of the same stock and is sharing the journey to an exciting – and now reassuring – new existence on a planet he has envisaged in his dreams.

AVAILABLE ON VIDEO IN UK ON *AMAZING STORIES 3* FROM CIC

FAMILY DOG

(1987)

Director: Brad Bird; *Script*: Brad Bird; *Animation Producers*: Brad Bird, Alexander V. King; *Animation Designer*: Tim Burton; *Animation Supervisor*: Chris Buck; *Editor*: Cynthia A. Haagens; *Associate Producer*: Cleve Reinhard; *Music*: Danny Elfmann, Steve Bartek

Voices of: Stan Freberg, Annie Potts, Mercedes McCambridge, Scott Menville, Brooke Ashley, Brad Bird, Marshall Efron, Stanley Ralph Ross, Jack Angel

An inventive animated comedy tale about the relationship of a family dog to the adults he manipulates.

AVAILABLE ON VIDEO IN UK ON *AMAZING STORIES 4* FROM CIC

Doc Emmett Brown (Christopher Lloyd) and Marty McFly (Michael J Fox) in *Back to the Future Part III*, 1990.

Selective Bibliography

BOB BALABAN, *Close Encounters of the Third Kind Diary*, New York, Paradise Press, 1977

ROBERT BLOCH, *Twilight Zone: The Movie* (novelization), New York, Warner Books, 1983

TERRY BROOKS, *Hook*, London, Arrow Books, 1992

TONY CRAWLEY, *The Steven Spielberg Story*, London, Zomba Books, 1983

SUSAN FREEMAN, *Indiana Jones and the Temple of Doom: Official Collector's Edition*, New York, Paradise Press, 1984

GEORGE GRIPE, *Gremlins* (novelization), New York, Avon Books, 1984

JAMES KAHN, *Indiana Jones and the Temple of Doom* (novelization), New York, Ballantine Books, 1984

WILLIAM KOTZWINKLE, *ET: The Extra-Terrestrial in His Adventures on Earth* (novelization), New York, Berkley Books, 1982

DONALD R. MOTT and CHERYL MCALLISTER SAUNDERS, *Steven Spielberg*, Boston, Twayne Publishers, 1986

MICHAEL PYE and LINDA MILES, *The Movie Brats*, New York, 1979

ROCHELLE REED, *The Sugarland Express*, Washington, 1974

NEIL SINYARD, *The Films of Steven Spielberg*, London, Bison Books, 1987

STEVEN SPIELBERG, *Close Encounters of the Third Kind* (novelization), New York, Dell, 1977

STEVEN SPIELBERG, *Letters to ET*, New York, Puttnams, 1983

DEREK TAYLOR, *The Making of Raiders of the Lost Ark*, New York, Ballantine Books, 1981

ALICE WALKER, *The Color Purple*, London, Women's Press Ltd, 1983

Interviews

Sugarland Express

A.C. Bobrow, 'The Sugarland Express: Interview'. *Filmmakers Newsletter*, Summer 1974

Jaws

Richard Combs, 'Primal Scream: an interview with Steven Spielberg', *Sight and Sound*, 46, 1977

Iain Johnstone, 'Steven Spielberg and the Great White Shark', *The Times*, 11 December 1985

Close Encounters of the Third Kind

Special edition of *American Cinematographer*, 59, 1978

Bruce Cook, 'Close Encounters with Steven Spielberg', *American Film*, November 1977

Jack Kroll, 'Close Encounters with Steven Spielberg', *Newsweek*, 21 November 1977

Gail Heathwood, 'Steven Spielberg', *Cinema Papers*, April/June, 1978

Mitch Tuchman, 'Close Encounters with Steven Spielberg', *Film Comment*, 14, 1978

1941

Special edition of *American Cinematographer*, 60, 1979

C. Hodenfield, '*1941*: Bombs Away!' *Rolling Stone*, 24 January 1980

David Reiss, '*1941*: A conversation with William A. Fraker', *Filmmakers Monthly*, 13, 1979

Raiders of the Lost Ark

Special edition of *American Cinematographer*, 62, 1981

David Reiss, '*Raiders of the Lost Ark*: An interview with Steven Spielberg', *Filmmakers Monthly*, 14, 1981

ET – The Extra-Terrestrial

Special edition of *American Cinematographer*, 64, 1983

Richard Corliss, 'I Dream for a Living', *Time*, 15 July 1985

Susan Royal, 'Steven Spielberg in his Adventures on Earth', *American Premiere*, 10 July 1982

Indiana Jones and the Temple of Doom

Nancy Griffin, 'Jungle Chums: Indy and Willie in a Race with Doom', *Life*, June 1984

The Color Purple

George Perry, 'Purple Raider', *Sunday Times*, 15 June 1986

Rodney Tyler, 'Close Encounters with Childhood', *The Times*, 23 November 1985

Empire of the Sun

Adam Pirani, 'J.G. Ballard: Abandoned Worlds, Fantasy Landscapes', *Starlog*, January 1988

Indiana Jones and the Last Crusade

Nancy Griffin, 'Spielberg's Last Crusade', *Time Out*, 24 May 1989

Innerspace

Interview with Joe Dante, *Starlog*, August 1987

Batteries Not Included

Carr D'Angelo, 'Mathew Robbins', *Starlog*, February 1988

Who Framed Roger Rabbit?

'Frank Marshall and his Latest Crusade', *Starlog*, December 1988

Hook

Fred Schroers; 'Peter Pandemonium' *Premiere*, December 1991

Ivor Davis and George Perry, 'Boys on the Never Never', *The Sunday Times*, 8 December 1991

General

Nigel Andrews 'Close Encounters of a Multimillion Kind', *Financial Times*, 3 February 1990

Kathryn M. Drennan, 'Kathleen Kennedy: Amblin Moviemaker', *Starlog*, February 1988

Bianca Jagger and Andy Warhol, 'Why Spielberg is simply out of this world', *Glasgow Herald*, 14 Decmber 1982

J. Moran, 'Interview with Steven Spielberg', *Cinema Papers*, July/August 1985

'Dialogue on Film: Steven Spielberg', *American Film*, June 1988

YOU Magazine, Interviews by David Lewin, March 1991

Richard Brooks, 'The Reel Peter Pan', *Sunday Times Magazine*, 29 March 1992

Index